# MAKE Clay Charms

Kaitlyn Nichols

**KLUTZ®**

**KLUTZ**® creates activity books and other great stuff for kids ages 3 to 103. We began our corporate life in 1977 in a garage we shared with a Chevrolet Impala. Although we've outgrown that first office, Klutz galactic headquarters is still staffed entirely by real human beings. For those of you who collect mission statements, here's ours:

● Create wonderful things   ● Be good   ● Have fun

## WRITE US

We would love to hear your comments regarding this or any of our books. We have many!

**KLUTZ**®
524 Broadway
5th Floor
New York, NY 10012
thefolks@klutz.com

We make Klutz books using resources that have been approved by the Forest Stewardship Council™. This means the paper in this book is made of material from well managed certified forests and other controlled sources.

FSC
www.fsc.org
**MIX**
Paper from
responsible sources
**FSC™ C113204**

Bracelets, jump rings, screw eye pins and glaze brush manufactured in China. All other parts, Taiwan. 85

©2013 Klutz. All rights reserved.
Published by Klutz, a subsidiary of Scholastic Inc.
Scholastic and associated logos are trademarks and/or registered trademarks of Scholastic Inc. Klutz and associated logos are trademarks and/or registered trademarks of Klutz. No part of this publication may be reproduced in any form or by any means without written permission of Klutz.

Distributed in Australia by Scholastic Australia Ltd
PO Box 579, Gosford, NSW, Australia 2250

Distributed in Canada by Scholastic Canada Ltd
604 King Street West, Toronto, Ontario, Canada M5V 1E1

Distributed in Hong Kong by Scholastic Hong Kong Ltd
Suites 2001-2, Top Glory Tower, 262 Gloucester Road
Causeway Bay, Hong Kong

ISBN 978-0-545-49856-2

8 8 8 0 7 5 8 5

### Safety Advice

- For ages 8 and up; store clay out of reach of young children and pets.
- Supervising adults should exercise discretion as to which activities are suitable and safe for children.
- The supervising adult should discuss the instructions and safety information with children before crafting.
- Protect work surface. Clays may stain or damage finished surfaces.
- The baking process should be carried out or supervised by an adult.
- Read and follow these instructions, safety rules, and first aid information and keep them for reference.
- It is best to craft in a clear area, away from food or drinks. The baking area should be well lit and ventilated. When clay charms are removed from the oven, they should be placed on a heat resistant counter or surface.
- Use only the tools that come with the kit or are recommended in the instructions.
- Wash hands after crafting.
- Clean all equipment after use.
- Do not exceed a temperature of 125˚C (260˚F). If baked at higher temperatures, the clay can release fumes which may irritate your eyes. If this happens, open the oven and windows and ventilate the area.
- Do not exceed a baking time of 30 minutes or the clay could burn.
- Do not use a microwave oven.
- In case the clay irritates your skin: Discontinue use and wash with soap or mild detergent. If reaction persists, seek immediate medical advice.
- Do not ingest the clay. In case of ingestion, drink water and contact your physician.

# CONTENTS

## Sweet Treats

19

20

21

22

23

24

25

26

28

## Good Eats

31

32

33

34

35

36

37

38

39

39

## Animals

41

42

43

44

45

45

46

47

48

50

## Beach

53

54

56

57

58

clay

You can make even more colors by mixing clay. (See page 10.)

This book comes with everything you need to make dozens of clay charms.

## Caring for Your Clay

Store your clay in resealable plastic bags so it doesn't dry out.

•

If your clay is a bit dry, roll it in your hands for a bit. The heat from your hands will warm up the clay and make it soft again.

•

If your clay is too soft, put it in a plastic bag in the fridge for 10 minutes. The cold air will firm it back up.

•

Before rolling a new color of clay, wash your hands with warm water and soap so any colored clay on your hands doesn't mix with the new clay.

•

Clay colors can stain. If you smear clay into your clothes or carpet, wash with warm water and soap right away.

clay shaping tool

The **flat side** makes shaping and flattening clay super simple.

The **knife edge** is great for cutting or unsticking clay from your work surface.

Use the **pointed end** to make small holes in your charms — like in the middle of mini doughnuts.

Clay Charms GLAZE .21 fl oz/ 6 ml

glaze

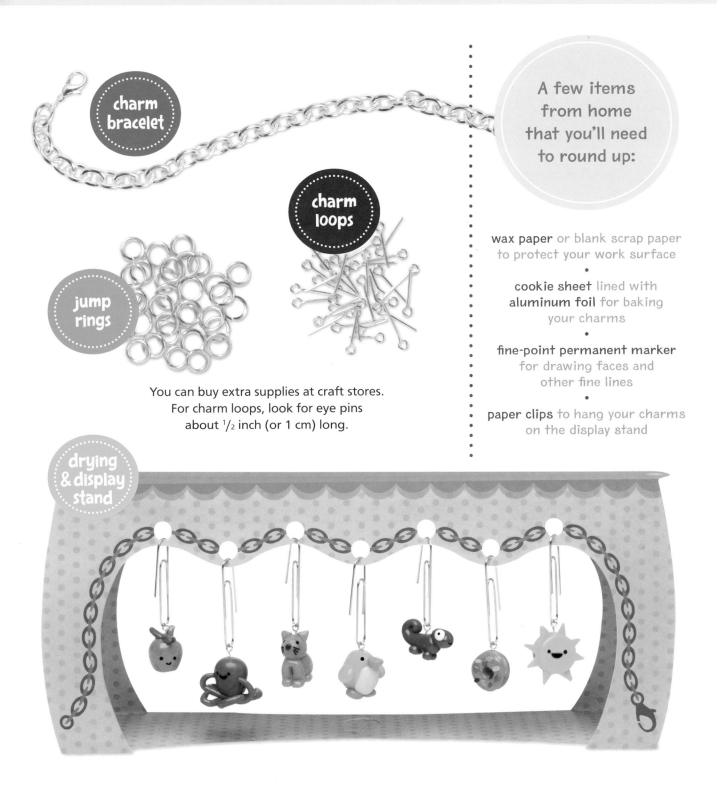

**charm bracelet**

**charm loops**

**jump rings**

You can buy extra supplies at craft stores.
For charm loops, look for eye pins
about $1/2$ inch (or 1 cm) long.

**A few items from home that you'll need to round up:**

**wax paper** or blank scrap paper to protect your work surface

**cookie sheet** lined with **aluminum foil** for baking your charms

**fine-point permanent marker** for drawing faces and other fine lines

**paper clips** to hang your charms on the display stand

**drying & display stand**

# CLAY BASICS

Before you start working with the clay, cover your work surface with a sheet of wax paper or scrap paper.

## At the beginning of each project,
there is a box that shows how many balls of clay you'll need in each color and exactly how big each ball should be:

Roll clay balls in these sizes and colors:

apple     leaves     stem

After you roll each ball, set it right on top of the picture to make sure you've got the size right.

- If the ball is too small, add a bit of clay and roll the ball until it's smooth.

- If the ball is too big, pinch off a bit of clay and roll it again.

THERE ARE ONLY 4 MOVES YOU NEED TO KNOW TO MAKE ALL THE CHARMS IN THIS BOOK: MAKING A BALL, ROLLING, FLATTENING, AND SHAPING.

## ✱ MAKING A BALL

Making the balls of clay shown at the beginning of each project is always the first step.

**big ball** To make a big ball of clay, tear off a bit of clay about as big as you want the ball to be. Roll the clay between your palms in a circular motion until it's nice and round. Easy.

**small ball** For a small ball, roll the clay between your thumb and index finger.

## ✱ ROLLING

Rolling a ball in different ways makes new shapes.

snake

thick snake

thin snake

Lay the ball on your work surface and use two fingers to roll it back and forth. The ball will turn into a snake. To make it the same thickness from end to end, use even pressure and roll your fingers over different parts of the snake as it gets longer.

oval

Place one finger on the middle of the ball and roll it back and forth once or twice.

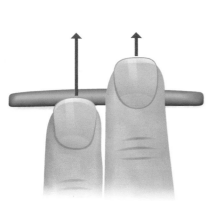

cone

Press your finger on one side of the ball and roll it back and forth three or four times.

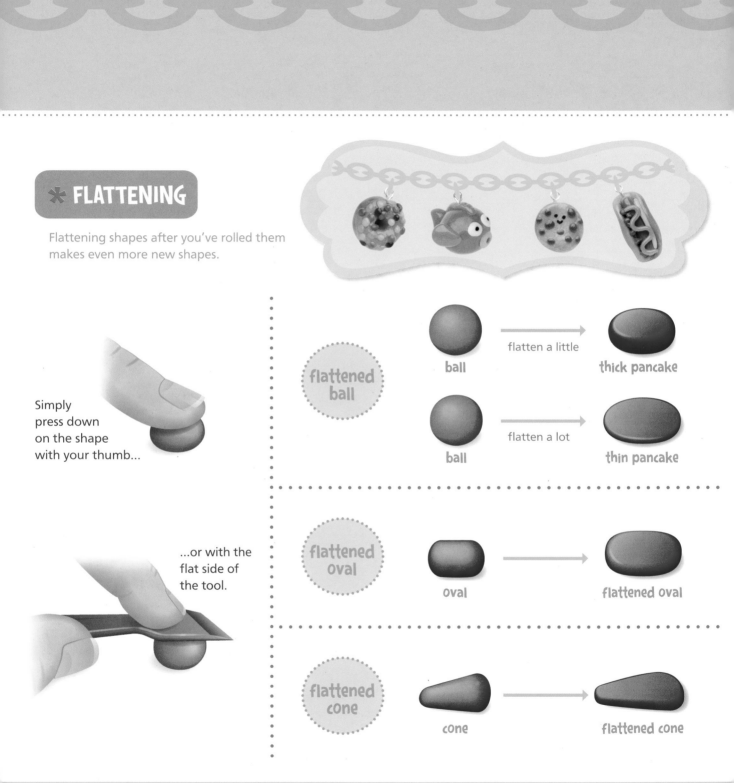

# ✳ FLATTENING

Flattening shapes after you've rolled them makes even more new shapes.

Simply press down on the shape with your thumb...

...or with the flat side of the tool.

**flattened ball**

ball → flatten a little → thick pancake

ball → flatten a lot → thin pancake

**flattened oval**

oval → flattened oval

**flattened cone**

cone → flattened cone

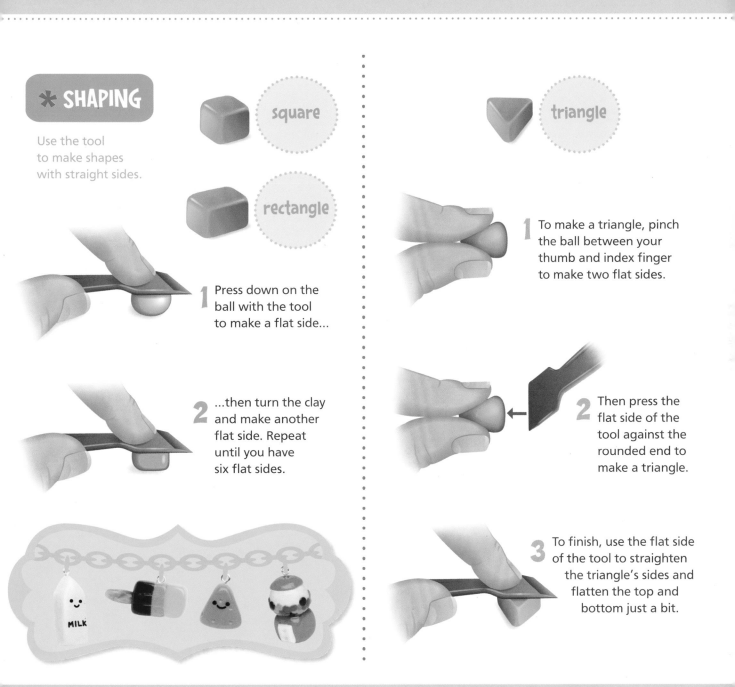

## ✳ SHAPING

Use the tool to make shapes with straight sides.

square

rectangle

1 Press down on the ball with the tool to make a flat side...

2 ...then turn the clay and make another flat side. Repeat until you have six flat sides.

MILK

triangle

1 To make a triangle, pinch the ball between your thumb and index finger to make two flat sides.

2 Then press the flat side of the tool against the rounded end to make a triangle.

3 To finish, use the flat side of the tool to straighten the triangle's sides and flatten the top and bottom just a bit.

## ✳ BLENDING COLORS

Choose your own colors for your charm, or make new clay colors by blending.

### CUSTOM CLAY COLORS

To create your own colors of clay, just mix two or three colors together. Start with a little bit of clay at first, then add small amounts to change the color more. Knead the clay colors between your fingers, roll them into a ball, then flatten and roll again. Keep kneading and rolling the clay until it is one even color.

There is no rule that says your lizard has to be green.

Follow the color & size guide below to make a whole new set of clay colors.

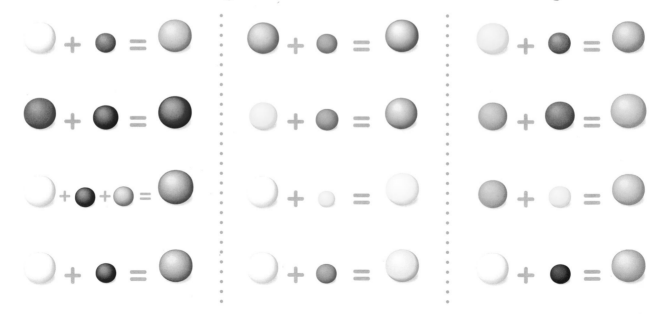

## ✳ UNIQUE ACCESSORIES

Before baking, add some basic clay shapes to your charm to make it completely your own.

### WINGS

**2 flattened cones**

Use the knife edge of the tool to make lines on the wings for feathers.

### TOP HAT

**oval**

**thin pancake**

A top hat at a bit of an angle makes any charm look dapper.

### BOW

cone    ball    cone

For a bow tie, press a bow under a chin (or a beak).

### COLLAR

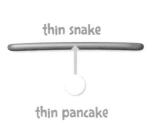

**thin snake**

**thin pancake**

Press the tag onto the collar, then wrap the collar around your charm's neck. Smooth out the crease where the ends of the collar meet.

# PUTTING YOUR CHARM TOGETHER

## ✳ ASSEMBLING CHARMS

These simple tips will help you put your charm together.

Don't press super hard when assembling your charm. A little tap with your finger will hold sprinkles on just fine.

Legs and wings may need a firmer push to stick to the body.

Use your finger to gently smooth out rough edges or creases.

## DON'T WORRY...

YOUR CHARM MAY NOT LOOK EXACTLY LIKE THE PICTURE — NO TWO CHARMS WILL COME OUT THE SAME. THAT'S PART OF WHAT MAKES THEM SO UNIQUELY ADORABLE.

## * ADDING CHARM LOOPS

The last step before baking is to add a charm loop.

**1** Hold your charm lightly with one hand. Press the pointed end of a charm loop all the way into the top of your charm...

**2** ...so the loop is facing the front like this:

### IF YOUR CHARM IS TOO THIN TO INSERT A CHARM LOOP...

**1** Press the charm loop onto the back of your charm.

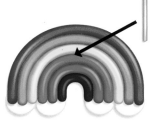

**2** Then press a thin pancake of clay over the pointed end...

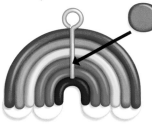

**3** ...so your charm looks like this:

## HOW YOUR CHARM HANGS IS REALLY UP TO YOU

You can hang your charm sideways, tilted, or even upside down if you like.

# BAKING & GLAZING

## ✳ BAKING YOUR CHARMS

Once you've added charm loops to your charms, you're ready to bake.

1. Line a cookie sheet with aluminum foil.

2. Make sure none of your charms are touching, but don't worry if things tip over.

3. Bake your creations in the oven at **250°F (120°C) for 20 minutes.** A small toaster oven works great, too. Do not use a microwave oven.

4. Keep an eye on your charms while they're baking. If you leave them in too long, the lighter colors may darken.

5. Wait for your charms to cool completely before handling (at least 15 minutes). Be extra careful with the metal charm loops — they may stay hot longer.

## ✳ DISPLAY STAND

While your charms are baking, set up your display stand. This is the perfect place to hang your glazed charms while they dry or to show off the charms you're not wearing.

1. Make sharp creases on all the fold lines.

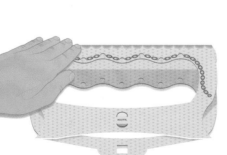

2. On the bottom, insert both tabs into the square slot, then flatten them.

## * DRAWING FACES

Add faces after you bake your charms but before you glaze them.

After baking, use a fine-point permanent marker to add faces to your animals, food, or any other charm creation.

**Nearly everything is cuter...**

**...when you add a little smiling face.**

Use your marker for details that are too small to be made out of clay.

## * GLAZING

Add a smooth shine to your charms for a finishing touch.

Poke one end of a paper clip through the charm loop. Hold the paper clip and brush a thin layer of glaze on your charm. It should be completely covered and shiny all over.

Pull the end of the paper clip out a bit, then hang your charm on the display stand. The glaze will be completely dry in about **30 minutes.**

# MAKING JEWELRY

## * CHARM BRACELET

When the glaze on your charms has dried, add them to your bracelet using jump rings.

**1** To open a jump ring, use your fingers to twist one side of the ring away from the other.

**2** Poke one end of the jump ring through the charm loop...

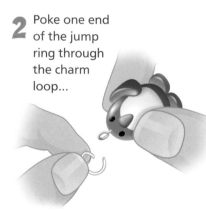

**3** ...and then through any link on your charm bracelet.

**4** Twist the jump ring again to close it.

## * REPAIRS

If the charm loop comes loose, coat it with a thin layer of glue and insert it back into the charm.

If a tentacle or a tail snaps off, you can repair your charm with a small dot of strong glue. Follow the instructions on the glue bottle.

Do not re-bake charms that have been glued.

# Other Ways to Wear Your Charms

## Pendant Necklace

To make a large pendant, double the size of each clay ball at the beginning of the project. Attach a jump ring to your charm and run some cord through it.

## Earrings

Use earring wires to turn small, lightweight charms into super-cute earrings.

## Zipper Charm

**1**  String 6 inches (15 cm) of cord through a jump ring attached to your charm. Tie the cord ends together in a knot.

**2** Pull the knotted end of the cord through the hole in your zipper.

**3** Drop your charm through the cord loop on the other side of the zipper.

**4** Lightly pull on the jump ring to tighten the cord. Be careful not to pull on the charm or the charm loop may come out.

# SWEET TREATS

# DOUGHNUT

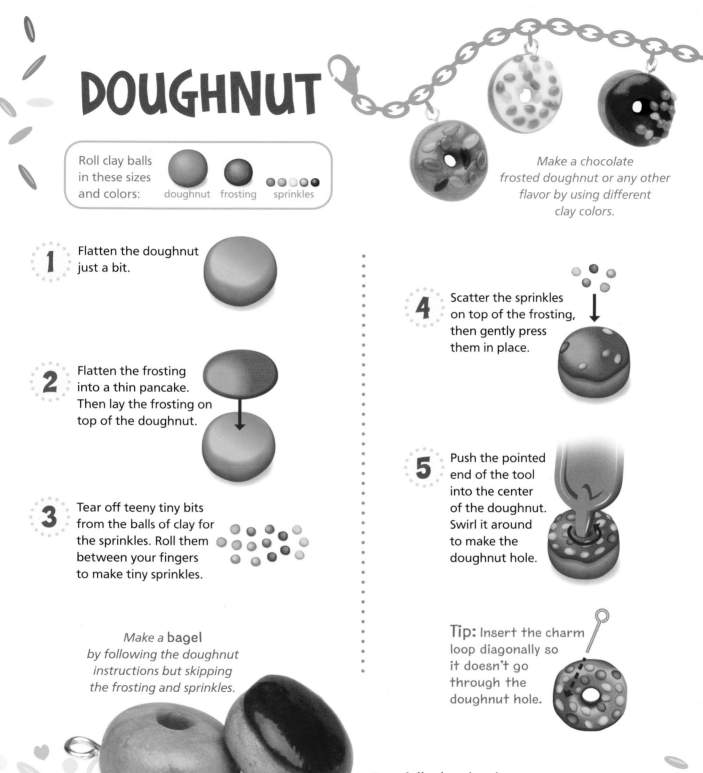

Roll clay balls in these sizes and colors:

doughnut    frosting    sprinkles

*Make a chocolate frosted doughnut or any other flavor by using different clay colors.*

**1** Flatten the doughnut just a bit.

**2** Flatten the frosting into a thin pancake. Then lay the frosting on top of the doughnut.

**3** Tear off teeny tiny bits from the balls of clay for the sprinkles. Roll them between your fingers to make tiny sprinkles.

**4** Scatter the sprinkles on top of the frosting, then gently press them in place.

**5** Push the pointed end of the tool into the center of the doughnut. Swirl it around to make the doughnut hole.

**Tip:** Insert the charm loop diagonally so it doesn't go through the doughnut hole.

*Make a **bagel** by following the doughnut instructions but skipping the frosting and sprinkles.*

*For a **jelly doughnut**, follow steps 1 and 2. Then add a small dot of pink clay on one side of your doughnut.*

19

# CINNAMON BUN

Roll clay balls in these sizes and colors: **dough** **cinnamon** **icing**

**1** Roll the dough and the cinnamon into snakes about this long:

**2** Press the two snakes together.

**3** Now hold the two snakes together and coil them all the way around the center.

*Press here.*

**4** Press the ends lightly against the coil to hold them in place.

**5** Roll the icing into a thin snake about this long:

**6** Lay the icing in a zigzag on top of the cinnamon bun.

# MILK & COOKIES

## MILK CARTON

Roll a clay ball in this size and color: milk carton

**1** Shape the milk carton into a rectangle. (See page 9 for the best way to do this.)

*Cut here.*

**2** Hold the sides of the milk carton and use the knife edge of the tool to cut off the two top corners.

**3** Use your fingers to smooth out the top of the carton so it looks like this:

**After baking,** write "MILK" on your carton and add a face if you like.

## CHOCOLATE CHIP COOKIE

Roll clay balls in these sizes and colors: cookie dough   chocolate

**1** Flatten the cookie dough into a pancake.

**2** Tear off teeny tiny bits from the ball of clay for the chocolate. Roll them between your fingers to make tiny chocolate chips.

**3** Scatter the chocolate chips across the top of the cookie...

**4** ...then lightly press them in place.

**Tip:** Press a charm loop onto the back of your cookie and cover with a thin pancake (see page 13).

# ICE POP

Roll clay balls in these sizes and colors:

*ice pop*    *stick*

# CREAM POP

Roll clay balls in these sizes and colors:

*pop*    *cream*    *stick*

**1** Press the three balls of clay for the ice pop together...

**1** Shape the orange pop into a rectangle. (See page 9 for the best way to do this.)

**2** ...then shape them into a rectangle. (See page 9 for the best way to do this).

*Flatten the sides with the tool.*

**2** Roll the cream into a thick snake and press it onto the bottom of the orange pop.

**3** Roll the stick into a thick snake, then press it firmly onto the bottom of the ice pop.

**3** Roll the stick into a thick snake and press it onto the bottom of the cream.

**4** Press lightly with the knife edge of your tool to make two lines on the ice pop. Flip over and repeat on the other side.

*To keep the rectangle shape, hold the sides of the ice pop while you make the lines.*

**After baking,** add a smiling face if you like.

# ICE-CREAM CONE

Roll clay balls in these sizes and colors:
cone  scoop  ring

**1** Roll the bronze clay into a cone shape.

**2** Press the flat side of the tool against the top of the cone to flatten it.

*Flatten here.*

**3** Lightly press the scoop onto the top of the cone.

**4** Roll the ring into a snake about this long:

**5** Wrap the snake around the bottom of the scoop, smoothing the ends together where they meet.

**6** Use the knife edge of the tool to make criss-crossing diagonal lines all around the cone.

## TOP IT OFF

**Sprinkles**
*Roll tiny bits of clay and gently press them onto the ice cream.*

**Double Scoop**
*Make an extra scoop and press it on top of the first one.*

**Soft Serve**
*Roll the scoop into a long snake. Wrap the snake around the top of the cone, then coil it on top.*

23

# LOLLIPOP

*Use different colored swirls for different lollipop flavors.*

Roll clay balls in these sizes and colors:
lollipop    stick

**1** Roll the balls of clay for the lollipop into snakes about this long:

**2** Press the two snakes together.

**3** Now hold one end of the snakes in place and gently twist the other end to make a swirl.

**4** Lightly roll the swirl on your work surface just enough to smooth it out.

**5** Hold one end of the swirl and coil the other end around to make the lollipop.

**6** Roll the stick into a thick snake, then press it firmly onto the lollipop where the coil ends.

**Tip:** If your lollipop is too thin to insert a charm loop, add the loop to the back as shown on page 13.

# GUMBALL MACHINE

Roll clay balls in these sizes and colors:

**gum** **bowl** **lid** **base** **coin slot**

**1** Tear off teeny tiny bits from the balls of clay for the gum. Roll them between your fingers to make tiny gumballs.

**2** Press the gumballs around the bottom half of the bowl.

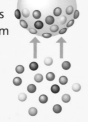

**3** Flatten the lid into a thin pancake. Press it onto the top of the bowl.

*Roll the bowl in your hands a few times to smooth everything out.*

**4** Next, use the tool to shape the base into a square. (See page 9 for the best way to do this.)

**5** Flatten the coin slot into a thin pancake. Then use the knife edge of the tool to cut the pancake into a rectangle.

Cut here.

**6** Press the coin slot onto the base.

**7** Use the pointed end of the tool to make two indents on the coin slot.

*Make two indents.*

**8** Now, lightly press the bowl onto the base.

25

# S'MORE

## GRAHAM CRACKERS

Roll clay balls in this size and color: **graham crackers**

**1** Flatten each of the graham crackers into a thin pancake.

**2** Use the knife edge of the tool to cut the pancakes into squares.

*Cut here.*

*The squares should be about the same size.*

**3** Next, use the knife edge to make a cross on each graham cracker.

**4** Use the pointed end of the tool to make four dots in each square of the graham crackers.

## CHOCOLATE

Roll a clay ball in this size and color: **chocolate**

**1** Flatten the chocolate into a thin pancake.

**2** Use the knife edge of the tool to cut the chocolate into a square the same size as the graham crackers.

*Cut here.*

**3** Use the knife edge to make a cross on the chocolate.

*To make a toasted marshmallow, mix a little bit of bronze clay into the white clay.*

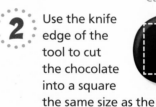

# MARSHMALLOW

Roll a clay ball in this size and color: **marshmallow**

**1** Roll the marshmallow into a thick snake, about this long:

**2** Squeeze the top and bottom of the snake to make a flattened marshmallow, perfect for stacking.

# PUT IT TOGETHER

To make the s'more, stack the ingredients on top of each other as shown below. Then lightly press down on the top graham cracker to hold it all in place.

*To make individual charms from the s'more ingredients, make two graham crackers and sandwich the charm loop in between. Do the same for the chocolate. Leave the marshmallow a bit taller.*

# CUPCAKE

Roll clay balls in these sizes and colors:
cake    frosting

*Switch up the colors of your cupcake and frosting to make different flavors.*

**1** Roll the cake into a thick cone.

**2** Lightly squeeze the top and bottom of the cone to flatten the cake.

**3** Shape the frosting by pushing down around the outside edge of the ball. It should look like this:

*A peak will form in the center.*

**4** Put the frosting on top of the cake.

**5** Use the knife edge of the tool to make lines all around the cake.

Happy Birthday!

# CUPCAKE DECORATION

## Swirl
Roll a long snake and coil it on top of the cake.

## Icing
Roll a small ball of clay into a thin snake and lay it over the frosting in a swirly shape.

## Rose
Hold one end of a short snake and coil the other end around to make a swirl.

## Carrot Cupcake
Roll a tiny ball of orange clay into a cone. Shape a tiny ball of green clay into a triangle.

## Sprinkles
Tear off tiny pieces of different-colored clay and roll them into balls. Drop them onto the frosting and push down lightly to secure.

GOOD EATS

# MACARONI & CHEESE

## MACARONI

Roll clay balls in these sizes and colors:

**blend**

macaroni

*For the best way to blend clay, see page 10.*

**1** Roll the macaroni into a snake.

**2** Curve the ends up a bit.

**3** Now, use the pointed end of the tool to make a hole in each end of the macaroni.

## CHEESE

Roll a clay ball in this size and color:

cheese

**1** Shape the cheese into a triangle. (See page 9 for the best way to do this.)

**2** Use the pointed end of the tool to make small holes for the cheese texture. Flip over and repeat on the other side.

**Best Friends Charms**
*Show your friend she's the cheese to your macaroni: Give her the cheese and you keep the macaroni.*

# CHEESEBURGER

Roll clay balls in these sizes and colors:

bun — lettuce — tomatoes — burger — cheese

**1** Flatten both pieces of the bun just a little bit. The thinner one will be the bottom bun.

**2** Next, flatten the lettuce into a thin pancake, just a bit larger than the bottom bun. Tear off the edges so the lettuce looks rough and leafy.

*Tear off the edges.*

**3** Flatten the tomatoes into thin pancakes.

**4** Now, flatten the burger into a thick pancake. Use the pointed end of the tool to make small dents all around the burger.

**5** Flatten the cheese into a thin pancake, then use the knife edge of the tool to cut it into a square.

*Cut here.*

**6** Stack the ingredients on top of each other as shown. Hold the edges of the top bun and lightly press down to hold it all together.

*For **sesame seeds**, scatter tiny bits of white clay over the top bun.*

32

# FRIES

Roll clay balls in these sizes and colors:
fries    bag

**1** Roll the fries into an oval, then flatten it into a pancake.

**2** Use the knife edge of the tool to make cuts in the top half of the fries.

**3** Next, roll the bag into a long oval and flatten it into a pancake.

*Make the bag long enough to wrap around the fries.*

**4** Wrap the bag around the bottom of the fries...

**5** ...then pinch the bottom of the bag closed. Smooth out the ends where they overlap, and shape the bag into a square.

*Smooth this edge.*

*Pinch along this edge.*

### Best Friends Charms
*Share your charms with your friend to let her know you two go together like a burger and fries.*

# HOT DOG

Roll clay balls in these sizes and colors:

| bun | | hot dog | | | mustard | relish | ketchup |
|-----|-----|-----|-----|-----|-----|-----|-----|
| | blend | | | | | | |

*For the best way to blend clay, see page 10.*

**1** Roll the bun into an oval, then flatten it into a thick pancake.

**2** Roll the hot dog into a thick snake, just a bit shorter than the bun.

**3** Lay the hot dog in the bun, then fold up the sides of the bun.

**4** Roll the mustard into a thin snake and lay it on one side of the hot dog.

**5** Tear off teeny tiny bits from the ball of clay for the relish. Roll them into balls and press them onto the other side of the hot dog.

**6** Roll the ketchup into a thin snake and lay it over the hot dog in a zig-zag shape.

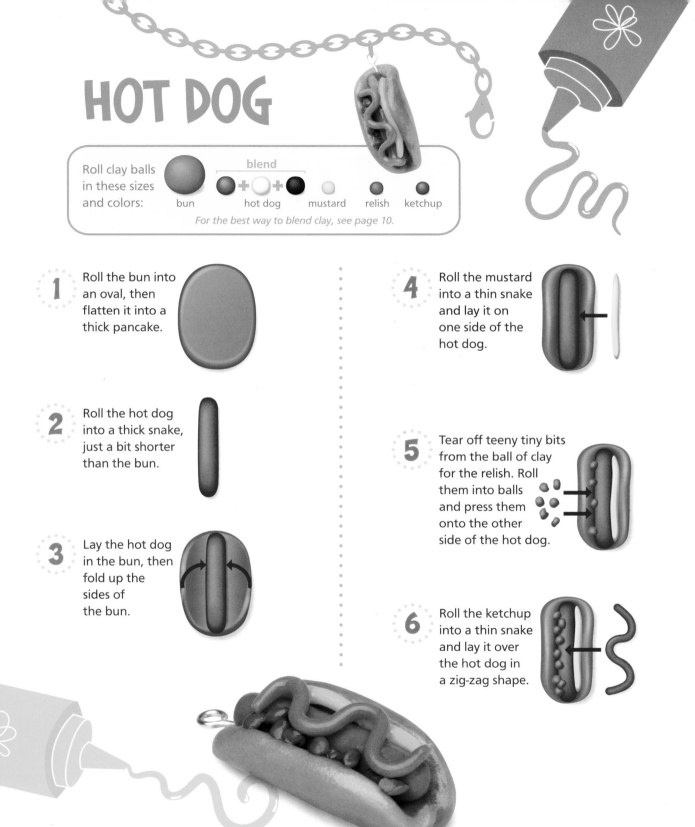

# TACO

**Roll clay balls in these sizes and colors:** tortilla  meat  lettuce  tomatoes  cheese

**1** Flatten the tortilla into a thin pancake.

**2** Tear off tiny bits from the ball of clay for the meat, then sprinkle them down the middle of the tortilla.

**3** Flatten the lettuce into a thin pancake, then tear off rough pieces and sprinkle over the meat.

**4** Roll the tomato into a snake, then tear off short pieces and sprinkle over the lettuce.

**5** Now do the same thing with the cheese. Roll it into a snake, then tear off short pieces and sprinkle on top of the tomatoes.

**6** Lightly press all the ingredients down so they don't fall out. Then fold up the sides of the tortilla.

**Tip:** Bake the taco on its side so the tortilla doesn't unfold.

35

# PEAS in a POD

Roll clay balls in these sizes and color: **pod** **peas** **vine**

**1** Flatten the pod into a thin pancake.

**2** Place the two peas in the middle of the pod.

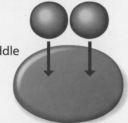

**3** Fold the top and bottom of the pod up around the peas...

**4** ...then pinch the ends together.

*Pinch here...*   *...and here.*

**5** Roll the vine into a thin snake, then lay it on one side of the pod in a curly shape.

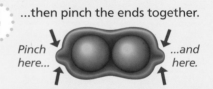

**After baking,** draw a face on each pea.

# CARROT

Roll clay balls in these sizes and colors:

carrot    leaves

**1** Roll the carrot into a cone.

**2** Next, roll the leaves into cones.

**3** Gather the leaves into a bunch, then press the thick ends onto the top of the carrot.

**4** Use the knife end of the tool to make little lines all around the carrot.

CARROTS

*To make a **bunch of carrots**, use less clay for each carrot, then press them together before baking.*

# APPLE

*Use a different clay color to make an apple of a different variety.*

Roll clay balls in these sizes and colors:

apple  leaves  stem

**1** Pinch the bottom of the apple just a bit, so it looks like the picture.

**2** Use the side of the tool to make a light indent across the top of the apple.

*The bottom of the apple will flatten just a bit.*

**3** Your apple should look like this from the side:

**4** Shape the leaves into triangles...

**5** ...then press them onto the top of the apple.

**6** Roll the stem into a thick snake and press it onto the top of the apple, behind the leaves.

*To make an **orange**, use an orange ball of clay and follow steps 4 and 5 for the apple.*

# PEAR

# STRAWBERRY

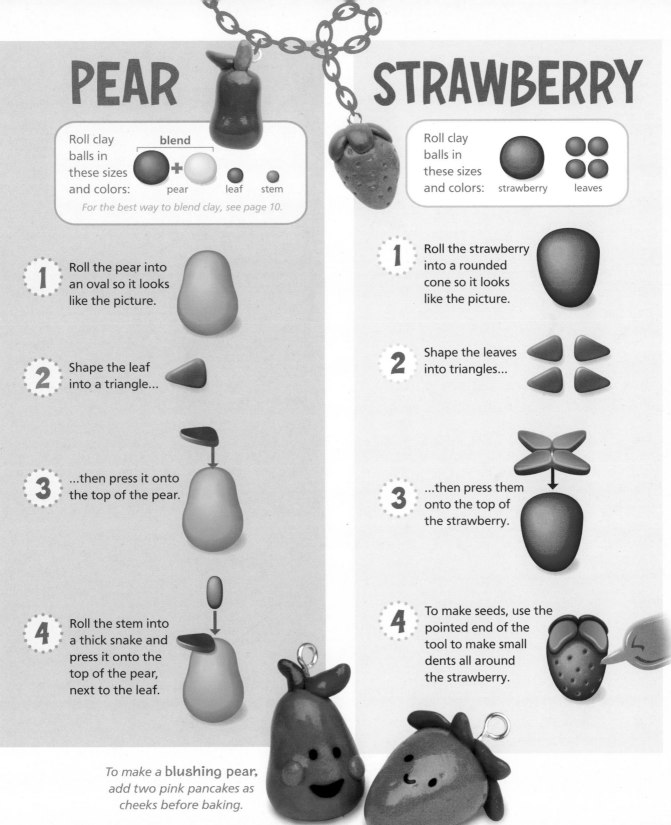

Roll clay balls in these sizes and colors: **blend** pear + leaf stem

*For the best way to blend clay, see page 10.*

Roll clay balls in these sizes and colors: strawberry leaves

**1** Roll the pear into an oval so it looks like the picture.

**1** Roll the strawberry into a rounded cone so it looks like the picture.

**2** Shape the leaf into a triangle...

**2** Shape the leaves into triangles...

**3** ...then press it onto the top of the pear.

**3** ...then press them onto the top of the strawberry.

**4** Roll the stem into a thick snake and press it onto the top of the pear, next to the leaf.

**4** To make seeds, use the pointed end of the tool to make small dents all around the strawberry.

*To make a **blushing pear,** add two pink pancakes as cheeks before baking.*

ANIMALS

# PIG

Roll clay balls in these sizes and color:

body    feet    snout    ears    tail

**1** Shape the body into a rectangle. (See page 9 for the best way to do this.)

**2** Lightly press each of the four feet onto the body.

**3** Now, stand up the pig. Press the snout onto the bottom of the face.

*The snout will flatten a bit.*

**4** Shape the ears into a triangles...

**5** ...then press them onto the front corners of the body.

**6** Roll the tail into a thin snake...

**7** ...then bend it into a curlicue. Lightly press one end onto the back of the pig.

**After baking,** draw two black eyes on the face and two short lines on the snout.

*To make your **pig** fly, check out the wings on page 11.*

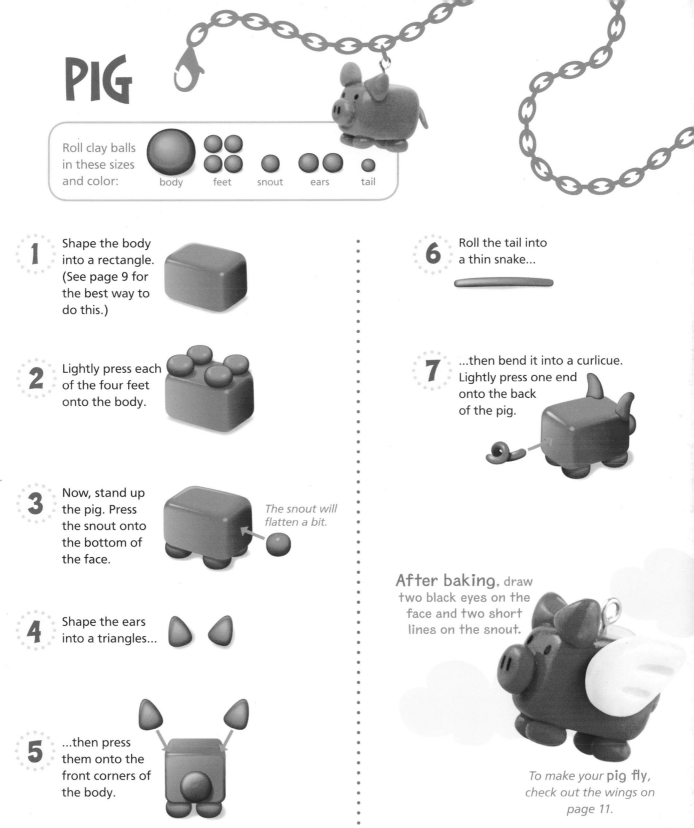

41

# GOLDFISH

Roll clay balls in these sizes and colors:

rim    bowl    tail    body    bubbles

**1** Roll the rim into a snake this long:

**2** Wrap the snake around the top of the bowl, smoothing the ends together where they meet.

*If your snake is too long, pinch off the extra. If your snake is too short, roll it a bit more so it gets longer.*

**3** To make the fish, roll the tail into a thick snake and flatten the body into a thick pancake.

**4** Bend the tail in half and press it onto the body...

*Flatten the tail to match the body.*

**5** ...then press the fish onto the bowl.

**6** Flatten the bubbles into pancakes, then press them onto the bowl in front of the fish.

**After baking,** draw a face on your goldfish.

# LIZARD

Roll clay balls in these sizes and colors:
**body**  **feet**  **head**  **eyes**

**1** Roll the body into a long cone.

**2** Lightly press each of the four feet onto the body.

**3** Now, stand up the lizard. Press the head firmly onto the front of the body.

**4** Flatten the eyes into pancakes, then press them onto either side of the head.

**5** Curl the lizard's tail up over its back.

After baking, draw a mouth on the head and add a black dot to each eye.

Add **spots** or **stripes** to your lizard if you want.

# HAMSTER

Roll clay balls in these sizes and colors:

body    head    feet    tail    ears    cheeks    nose

**1** Press the head onto the body.

**2** Lightly press each of the four feet onto the body.

**3** Now stand up the hamster. Press the tail onto the back of the body.

*The feet will flatten a bit.*

**4** Press the ears onto the top of the head.

**5** Next, flatten each of the cheeks into pancakes, then press them onto the bottom of the head so they are touching.

**6** Press the nose onto the head, right above the cheeks.

**After baking,** draw two eyes on your hamster.

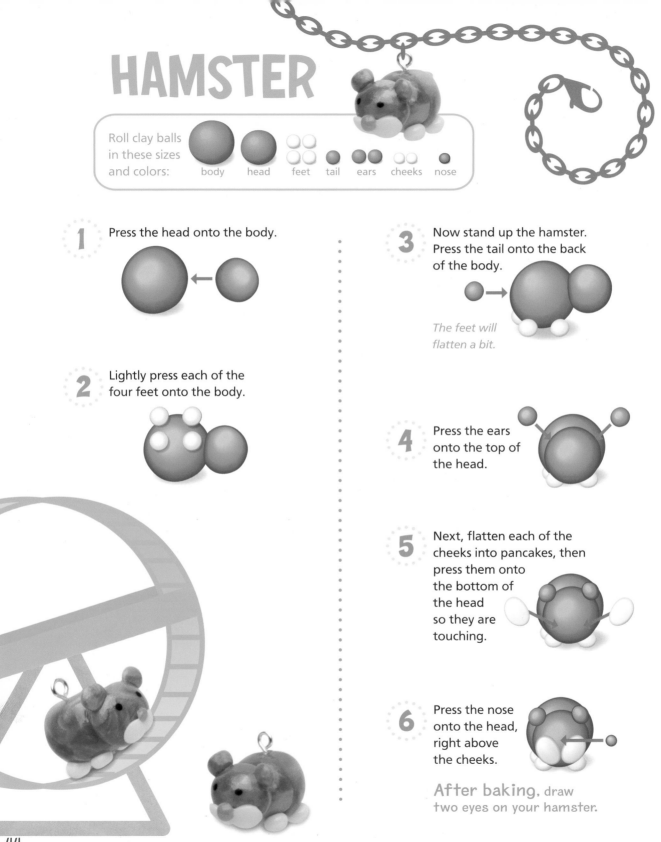

# BUNNY

Roll clay balls in these sizes and colors:

body  head  feet  tail
ears  cheeks  nose

**1** Assemble the bunny's body, head, feet, and tail by following steps 1–3 for the hamster on page 44.

**2** Roll the ears into thick snakes...

**3** ...then press them onto the top of the head.

**4** Follow steps 5 and 6 for the hamster to add the cheeks and nose.

**After baking,** draw two eyes on your bunny.

*Make a **floppy-eared bunny** by flattening the ears, then attaching them to the sides of the head.*

# MOUSE

Roll clay balls in these sizes and colors:

body  head  feet  tail
ears  nose

**1** Assemble the mouse's body, head, and feet by following steps 1 and 2 for the hamster on page 44.

**2** Roll the tail into a snake...

**3** ...then press it onto the back of the mouse in an "s" shape.

**4** Flatten the ears into pancakes, then press them onto the head.

**5** Now, press the nose onto the front of the head.

**After baking,** draw two eyes on your mouse.

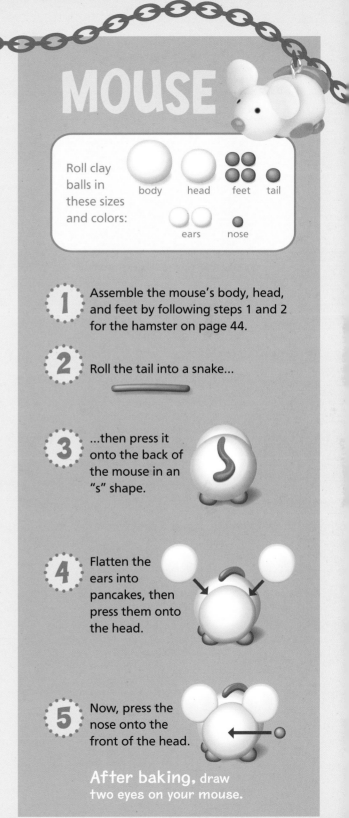

# DOG

Roll clay balls in these sizes and colors:

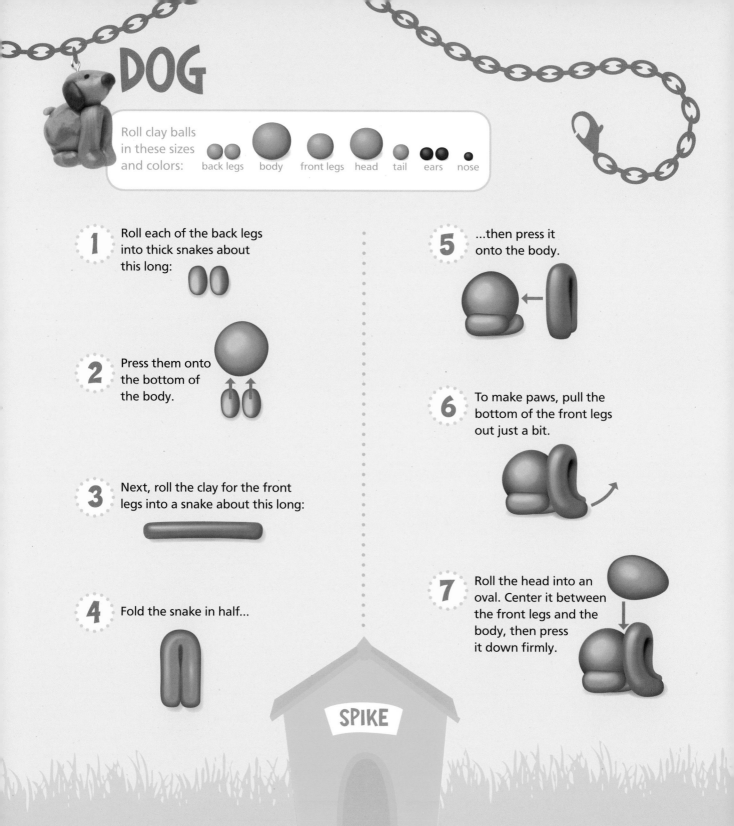

back legs    body    front legs    head    tail    ears    nose

**1** Roll each of the back legs into thick snakes about this long:

**2** Press them onto the bottom of the body.

**3** Next, roll the clay for the front legs into a snake about this long:

**4** Fold the snake in half...

**5** ...then press it onto the body.

**6** To make paws, pull the bottom of the front legs out just a bit.

**7** Roll the head into an oval. Center it between the front legs and the body, then press it down firmly.

SPIKE

46

**8** Now, roll the tail into a snake. Bend it slightly, then press it onto the back of the body.

**9** Roll the ears into ovals, then flatten them into pancakes. Press them onto either side of the head.

**10** Press the nose onto the front of the head.

*The nose will flatten a bit.*

**After baking,** draw on eyes.

*Give your dog a **collar**. (See page 11.)*

*Dress up your kitty with a **bow**. (See page 11.)*

# CAT

Roll clay balls in these sizes and colors:

back legs    body

front legs    head    tail    ears    nose

**1** Assemble the cat by following steps 1–7 for the dog on page 46.

**2** Shape the ears into triangles. (See page 9 for the best way to do this.)

**3** Press the ears onto either side of the head.

**4** Now, shape the nose into a triangle and press it onto the front of the head.

**After baking,** draw on eyes and whiskers.

# PENGUIN

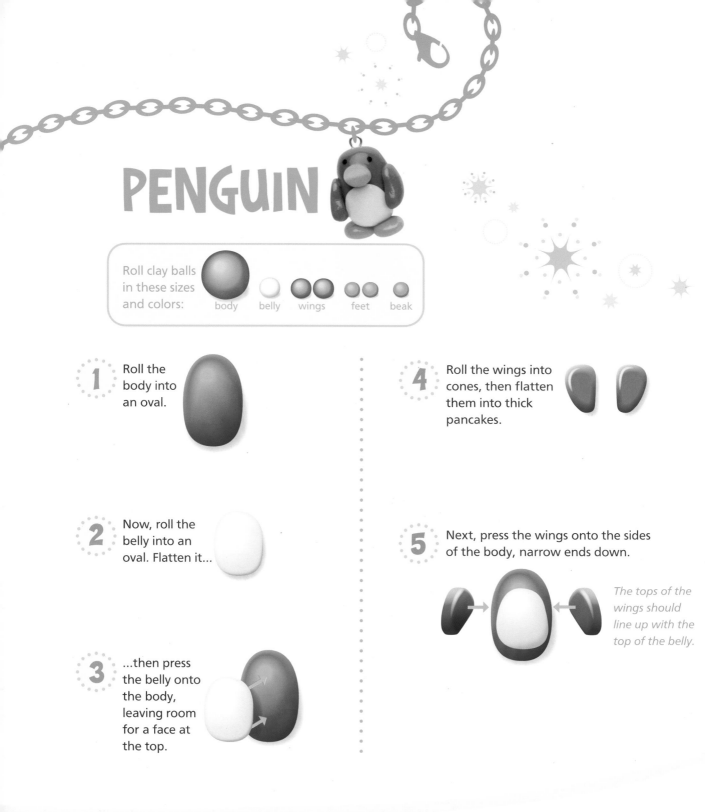

Roll clay balls in these sizes and colors:

body   belly   wings   feet   beak

**1** Roll the body into an oval.

**2** Now, roll the belly into an oval. Flatten it...

**3** ...then press the belly onto the body, leaving room for a face at the top.

**4** Roll the wings into cones, then flatten them into thick pancakes.

**5** Next, press the wings onto the sides of the body, narrow ends down.

*The tops of the wings should line up with the top of the belly.*

**6** Flatten the feet into thick pancakes, then press them onto the bottom of the body.

**7** Roll the beak into a cone, then press it onto the body right above the belly.

**After baking,** draw eyes above the beak.

To make a **chick**, swap the blue clay for yellow and shorten the wings a tad.

SOUTH POLE

Dress up your penguin with a **bow tie**. (See page 11.)

# OWL

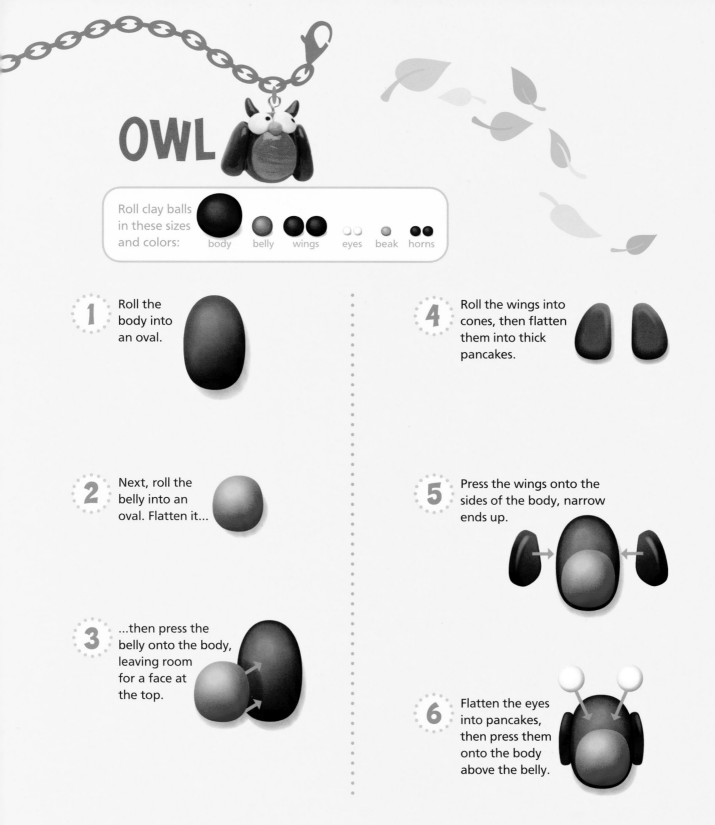

Roll clay balls in these sizes and colors:

body  belly  wings  eyes  beak  horns

**1** Roll the body into an oval.

**2** Next, roll the belly into an oval. Flatten it...

**3** ...then press the belly onto the body, leaving room for a face at the top.

**4** Roll the wings into cones, then flatten them into thick pancakes.

**5** Press the wings onto the sides of the body, narrow ends up.

**6** Flatten the eyes into pancakes, then press them onto the body above the belly.

**7** Roll the beak into a cone, then press it onto the body below the eyes.

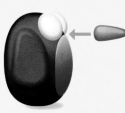

**8** Now, roll the two horns into tiny cones. Press them onto the body above each eye.

**9** Use the knife edge of the tool to make feather lines on the belly and wings.

**After baking,** draw a black dot on each of the eyes.

*To make a **parrot**, follow steps 1–7 for the owl using brightly colored clay.*

BEACH

# SUN

Roll clay balls in these sizes and color:

middle   bottom   top

**1** Flatten the middle, bottom, and top of the sun into pancakes.

*They should all be about the same thickness.*

**2** Use the knife edge of the tool to cut the middle piece into the shape of a sun. Aim for six or seven points — don't worry if it's not perfect.

Cut here. ———

**3** Stack the pieces on top of each other as shown.

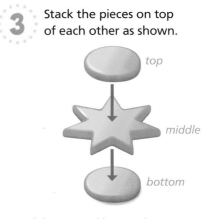

top

middle

bottom

*If the top and bottom layers are covering too much of the middle, tear a bit off of the top and bottom pancakes and flatten them again.*

**Tip:** Insert the charm loop between the middle and bottom layers.

**After baking,** draw a smiley face on both sides of your sun.

# FISH

Roll clay balls in these sizes and colors:

**body**    **eyes**    **fins**    **tail**    **lips**

**1** Flatten each eye into a pancake, then press them onto either side of the body as shown.

**2** Roll the fins into ovals, then flatten them into pancakes.

**3** Press the fins onto the sides of the body.

**4** Roll the tail into a thick snake about this long:

**5** Bend the snake in half...

**6** ...then press it onto the back of the body.

*To make snorkeling gear, roll two long snakes and shape them into a mask and snorkel.*

*Make a* **school of fish** *by mixing and matching different colors, fins, and faces.*

**7** Now, roll the lips into a thick snake about this long:

**8** Bend the snake in half, then press it onto the body below the eyes.

**After baking,** draw a black dot on each eye.

Big mouth

Mohawk

Fancy fins

Stripes

# CRAB

Roll clay balls in these sizes and colors:

body   legs   claws   eyes

**1** Flatten the body into a thick pancake.

**2** Roll each leg into a snake about this long:

**3** Press the legs onto the middle of the body so they look like this:

*Pull the ends of the legs apart.*

**4** Flatten the claws into thick pancakes, then press them onto the body in front of the legs.

**5** Now, flip the crab over. Use the knife edge of the tool to make cuts down the centers of the claws.

*Cut here...*          *...and here.*

**6** Flatten the eyes into thick pancakes, then press them onto the top of the body so they stand up.

After baking, draw a black dot on each eye.

# OCTOPUS

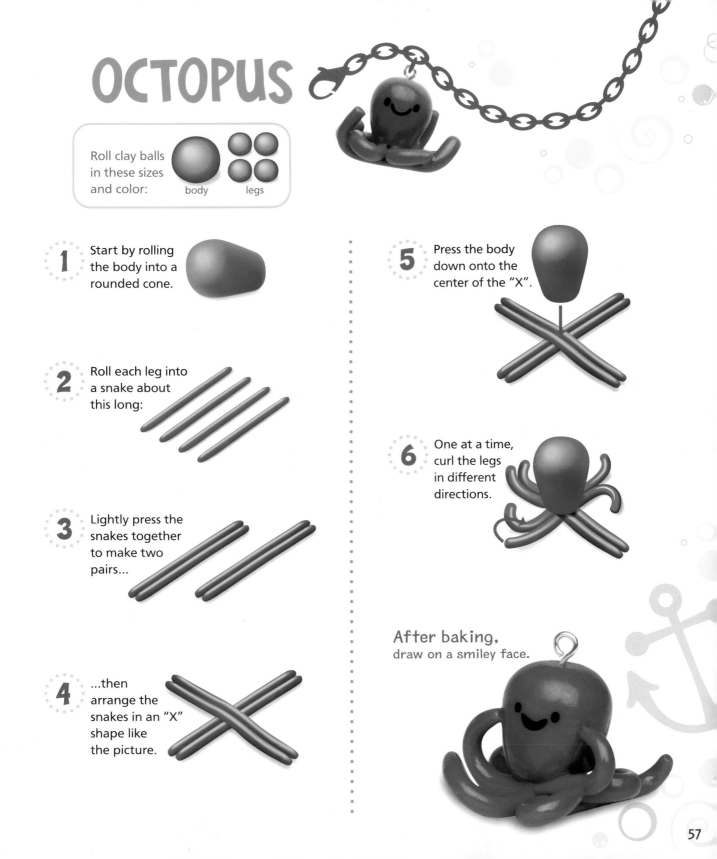

Roll clay balls in these sizes and color:

body    legs

**1** Start by rolling the body into a rounded cone.

**2** Roll each leg into a snake about this long:

**3** Lightly press the snakes together to make two pairs...

**4** ...then arrange the snakes in an "X" shape like the picture.

**5** Press the body down onto the center of the "X".

**6** One at a time, curl the legs in different directions.

After baking, draw on a smiley face.

# RAINBOW

Roll clay balls in these sizes and colors:

rainbow    clouds

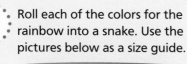

**1** Roll each of the colors for the rainbow into a snake. Use the pictures below as a size guide.

**2** Bend the purple snake into a small arch.

**3** Wrap the blue snake over the top of the purple arch.

**4** Continue wrapping each longer snake around the arches to make a rainbow.

*Don't worry if the ends of the snakes don't line up perfectly. You can trim them with the knife edge of the tool.*

**5** Press three of the balls of clay for the clouds together. Do the same with the other three balls.

**6** Flatten the clouds just a bit...

**7** ...then press them onto each end of the rainbow.

**8** Now, flip the rainbow over. Lightly press a charm loop onto the back of the rainbow.

*If your charm sticks to your work surface, free it by gently sliding the flat side of the tool underneath it.*

**9** Press a thin pancake over the pointed end of the charm loop to hold it in place.

**After baking,** draw a smiley face on each cloud.

# Credits

**Designer**
Jenna Nybank

**Art Director**
Maria Corrales

**Editor**
Anne Akers Johnson

**Instructional Illustrators**
Jim Kopp, Quillon Tsang

**Decorative Illustrator**
Andi Butler

**Photographer**
Joseph Quever

**Package and Display Stand Designer**
David Avidor

**Clay Tool Designer**
Quillon Tsang

**Production Editor**
Jen Mills

**Production Coordinator**
Mimi Oey

**Editorial Assistant**
Rebekah Lovato Piatte

**Clay Crafting Assistants**
Jenna Nybank, Suzie Poulson, Madeleine Robins, Kiele Gregoire, Eleanor Hanson Wise

Thanks to Eva Steele-Saccio for her charming idea and to all the project testers at Klutz for making a bazillion charms.

## Get creative with more from KLUTZ®

Looking for more goof-proof activities, sneak peeks, and giveaways? Find us online!

 KlutzCertified    KlutzCertified    KlutzCertified    KlutzCertified    Klutz

Klutz.com • thefolks@klutz.com • 1-800-737-4123

# INFORMANIA
# GHOSTS

## by Christopher Maynard

# About This Book

Ghosts got you? They will soon!
Here's everything you ever wanted to know about
these spooky specters—maybe even things
you'd rather not know. Prepare to be scared!

## Section 1 . . . page 5
## A Ghost Story

In an empty house on an empty
street, two people are searching,
room by room, by the light of
a small candle, for the ghost
of a murderer. Follow them if
you dare, in a horribly scary
story from my haunted library.

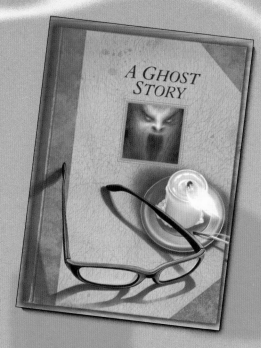

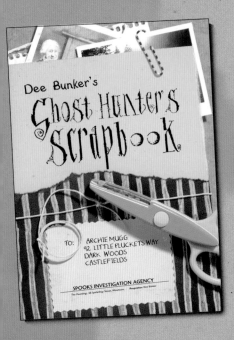

## Section 2 . . . page 21
## How To Catch a Ghost

Before you go looking for ghosts,
you'd better read this. Veteran
ghost hunter Dee Bunker shares
her top tips on what to look for
and where as she revisits some
of her favorite cases.

## Section 3 . . . page 47
## Find the Fakes

Ever seen a ghost and then realized it was your best friend in an old sheet? Join the museum tour that exposes the world's sneakiest hoaxes. With so many phony phantoms around, it's hard to believe in the real thing.

## Section 4 . . . page 63
## Ghosts at the Movies

Movie mogul Michael Johnstone has sent me a movie guide for FRIGHT NIGHT, a special screening of great ghost movies at his local theater. I don't know whether I'm too scared to go or not.

## Ready Reference . . . page 79

Finally, to help you sort out the facts behind the fiction, here's a Haunted History, a Map, Internet listings, a Glossary, and an Index.

*Christopher Obymond*

# About The Authors

**C**hris Maynard (only his mother calls him Christopher) would love to meet a ghost one day. He expects to come back as a ghost himself, to plague his noisy neighbors. Meanwhile he is busy writing for children. In 1998 he received the Oppenheim Toy Portfolio Gold Seal, for his INFORMANIA: SHARKS.

**M**ichael Johnstone's interest in ghosts dates back to when he and his brother spent a night in a haunted house and their dog refused to enter the room they slept in. Some time later he saw his first ghost, in A CHRISTMAS CAROL in a movie theater. He has been going to and writing about the movies ever since.

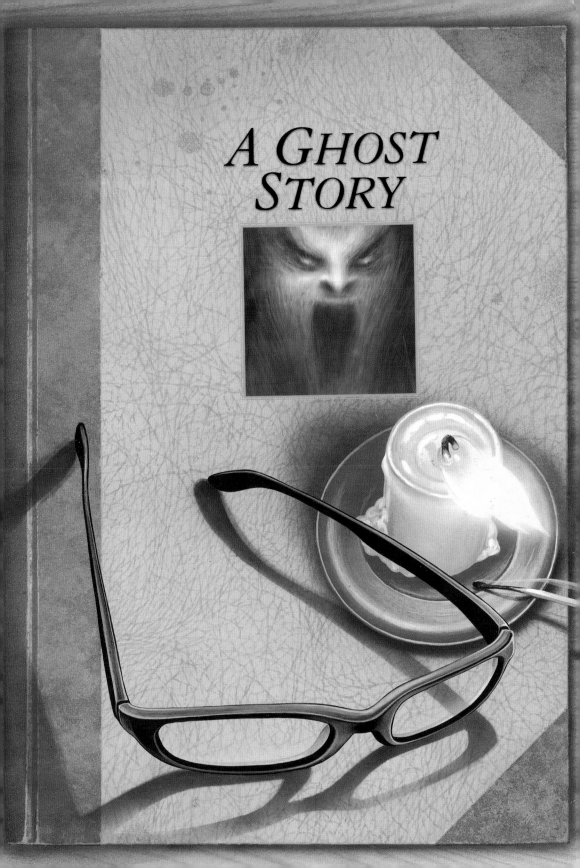

# ABOUT
## THIS STORY

Have you ever been scared
by words? Specially abridged for
*INFORMANIA* readers, *The Empty
House* is fourteen pages of pure
terror! Read it if you dare . . .

Author Algernon Blackwood
(1869–1951) had an extraordinary
life. Perhaps that's why he wrote
extraordinary stories. As a young
man he traveled far and wide,
tried his hand at many jobs (from
farming to bartending), failed
at all of them, and almost starved
in New York. Finally he came
home to England and started to
write. His first book contained
the story you are about to read.
More followed, and Blackwood
was hailed as one of the
great masters of horror.

CANDLEWICK PRESS

# THE EMPTY HOUSE

A TALL, NARROW HOUSE rose before them into the night, ugly in shape and painted a dingy white. Shutterless windows, without blinds, stared down upon them, shining here and there in the moonlight. There were weather streaks in the wall and cracks in the paint, and the balcony bulged out from the first floor a little unnaturally. But, beyond this generally forlorn appearance of an unoccupied house, there was nothing at first sight to single out this particular mansion for the evil character it had most certainly acquired.

Taking a look over their shoulders to make sure they had not been followed, they went boldly up the steps and stood against the huge black door that fronted them forbiddingly. But the first wave of nervousness was now upon them, and Shorthouse fumbled a long time with the key before he could fit it into the lock at all. A stray puff of wind wandering down the empty street woke a momentary rustling in the trees behind them, but otherwise this rattling of the key was the only sound audible; and at last it turned in the lock and the heavy door swung open and revealed a yawning gulf of darkness beyond.

With a last glance at the moonlit square, they passed quickly in and the door slammed behind them with a roar that echoed through empty halls and passages. But, instantly, with the echoes, another sound made itself heard.

A man had coughed close beside him — so close that it seemed they must have been actually by his side in the darkness. Shorthouse at once swung his heavy stick in the direction of the sound; but it met nothing more solid than air.

He heard his aunt give a little gasp beside him.

"There's someone here," she whispered; "I heard him."

"Be quiet!" he said sternly. "It was nothing but the noise of the front door."

"Oh! get a light—quick!" she added, as her nephew, fumbling with a box of matches, let them all fall with a rattle onto the stone floor.

The sound, however, was not repeated; and there was no evidence of retreating footsteps. In another minute they had a candle burning, using an empty end of a cigar case as a holder; and when the first flare had died down he held the impromptu lamp aloft and surveyed the scene.

They were standing in a wide hallway; on their left was the open door of a spacious dining room, and in front the hall ran, ever narrowing, into a long, dark passage that led apparently to the top of the kitchen stairs. The broad uncarpeted staircase rose in a sweep before them, everywhere draped in shadows, except for a single spot about halfway up where the moonlight came in through the window and fell in a bright patch on the boards. As Shorthouse peered up into the well of darkness and thought of the countless empty rooms and passages in the upper part of the old house, he caught himself longing again for the safety of the moonlit square, or the cozy, bright drawing room they had left an hour before. Then realizing that these thoughts were dangerous, he thrust them away again and summoned all his energy for concentration on the present.

"Aunt Julia," he said aloud, severely, "we must now go through the house from top to bottom and make a thorough search."

The echoes of his voice died away slowly all over the building, and in the intense silence that followed he turned to look at her. In the candlelight he saw that her face was

already ghastly pale; but she dropped his arm for a moment and said in a whisper, stepping close in front of him—

"I agree. We must be sure there's no one hiding. That's the first thing."

Arm in arm, Shorthouse holding the dripping candle and the stick, while his aunt carried the cloak over her shoulders, figures of utter comedy to all but themselves, they began a systematic search.

~ ❧ ~

Stealthily, walking on tiptoe and shading the candle lest it should betray their presence through the shutterless windows, they went first into the big dining room. There was not a stick of furniture to be seen. Bare walls, ugly mantelpieces, and empty grates stared at them. Everything, they felt, resented their intrusion; whispers followed them; shadows flitted noiselessly to right and left; something seemed ever at their back, watching, waiting for an opportunity to do them injury.

Out of the gloomy dining room they passed through large folding doors into a sort of library or smoking room, wrapped equally in silence, darkness, and dust; and from this they regained the hall near the top of the back stairs.

Here a pitch black tunnel opened before them into the lower regions, and—it must be confessed—they hesitated. But only for a minute. With the worst of the night still to come it was essential to turn from nothing.

"Come on!" he said peremptorily, and his voice ran on and lost itself in the dark, empty spaces below.

"I'm coming," she faltered, catching his arm with unnecessary violence.

They went a little unsteadily down the stone steps, a cold, damp air meeting them in the face, close and malodorous. The kitchen, into which the stairs led along a narrow passage, was large, with a lofty ceiling. Several doors opened out of it—some into cupboards with empty jars still standing on the shelves, and others into horrible little ghostly back offices, each colder and less inviting than the last. Black beetles scurried over the floor, and once, when they knocked against a table, something about the size of a cat jumped down with a rush and fled across the stone floor into the darkness. Everywhere there was a sense of recent occupation, an impression of sadness and gloom.

Leaving the main kitchen, they next went toward the scullery. The door was standing ajar, and as they pushed it open to its full extent Aunt Julia uttered a piercing scream, which she instantly tried to stifle by placing her hand over her mouth. For a second Shorthouse stood stock-still, catching his breath. He felt as if his spine had suddenly become hollow and someone had filled it with particles of ice.

Facing them, directly in their way between the doorposts, stood the figure of a woman. She had disheveled hair and wildly staring eyes, and her face was terrified and white as death.

She stood there motionless for the space of a single second. Then the candle flickered and she was gone—gone utterly—and the door framed nothing but empty darkness.

"Only the beastly jumping candlelight," he said quickly, in a voice that sounded like someone else's and was only half under control. "Come on, aunt. There's nothing there."

With a clattering of feet and a great appearance of boldness they went on, but over his body the skin moved as if crawling ants covered it. The scullery was cold, bare, and empty; more like a large prison cell than anything else. They went around it, tried the door into the yard, and the windows, but found them all fastened securely.

"There's nothing here, aunty," he repeated aloud quickly.

"Let's go upstairs and see the rest of the house. Then we'll choose a room to wait up in."

She followed him obediently, keeping close to his side, and they locked the kitchen door behind them. It was a relief to get upstairs again. In the hall there was more light than before, for the moon had traveled a little farther down the stairs. Cautiously they began to go up into the dark vault of the upper house, the boards creaking under their weight.

On the first floor they found the large double drawing room, a search of which revealed nothing. Here also was no sign of furniture or recent occupancy; nothing but dust and neglect and shadows. They opened the big folding doors between front and back drawing room and then came out again to the landing and went on upstairs. They had not gone up more than a dozen steps when they both simultaneously stopped to listen, looking into each other's eyes with a new apprehension across the flickering candle flame. From the room they had left hardly ten seconds before came the sound of doors quietly closing. It was beyond all question; they heard the booming noise that accompanies the shutting of heavy doors, followed by the sharp catching of the latch.

"We must go back and see," said Shorthouse briefly, in a low tone, and turning to go downstairs again.

When they entered the front drawing room it was plain that the folding doors had been closed—half a minute before. Without hesitation Shorthouse opened them. He almost expected to see someone facing him in the back room; but only darkness and cold air met him. They went through both rooms, finding nothing unusual. They tried in every way to make the doors close of themselves, but there was not wind enough even to set the candle flame flickering. The doors would not move without strong pressure. All was silent as the grave. Undeniably the rooms were utterly empty, and the house utterly still.

13

"It's beginning," whispered a voice at his elbow which he hardly recognized as his aunt's.

He nodded, taking out his watch to note the time. It was fifteen minutes before midnight; he made the entry of exactly what had occurred in his notebook, setting the candle in its case upon the floor in order to do so. It took a moment or two to balance it safely against the wall.

Aunt Julia always declared that at this moment she was not actually watching him, but had turned her head toward the inner room, where she fancied she heard something moving; but, at any rate, both positively agreed that there came a sound of rushing feet, heavy and very swift — and the next instant the candle was out!

But to Shorthouse himself had come more than this. For, as he rose from the stooping position of balancing the candle, and before it was actually extinguished, a face thrust itself forward so close to his own that he could almost have touched it with his lips. It was a face working with passion; a man's face, dark, with thick features, and angry, savage eyes.

In spite of himself, Shorthouse uttered a little cry, nearly losing his balance as his aunt clung to him in one moment of real, uncontrollable terror. Fortunately, however, she had seen nothing, but had only heard the rushing feet, for her control returned almost at once, and he was able to disentangle himself and strike a match.

The shadows ran away on all sides before the glare, and his aunt stooped down and groped for the cigar case with the precious candle. Then they discovered that the candle had not been *blown* out at all; it had been *crushed* out. The wick was pressed down into the wax, which was flattened as if by some smooth, heavy instrument.

How his companion so quickly overcame her terror, Shorthouse never properly understood. Equally inexplicable to him was the evidence of physical force they had just witnessed. He at once suppressed the memory of stories he had heard of "physical mediums"; for if these were true, and either his aunt or himself was unwittingly a physical medium, it meant that they were simply aiding to focus the forces of a haunted house already charged to the brim. It was like walking with unprotected lamps among uncovered stores of gunpowder.

So, with as little reflection as possible, he simply relit the candle and went up to the next floor. The arm in his trembled, it is true, and his own tread was often uncertain, but they went on with thoroughness, and after a search revealed nothing they climbed the last flight of stairs to the top floor of all.

Here they found a perfect nest of small servants' rooms, with broken pieces of furniture, dirty cane-bottomed chairs, cracked mirrors, and decrepit bedsteads. The rooms had low sloping ceilings hung here and there with cobwebs, small windows, and badly plastered walls — a depressing and dismal region which they were glad to leave behind.

～ ❧ ～

It was on the stroke of midnight when they entered a small room on the third floor, close to the top of the stairs, and arranged to make themselves comfortable for the remainder of their adventure. It was said to be the room — then used as a clothes closet — into which the infuriated groom had chased his victim and finally caught her. Outside, across the narrow landing, began the stairs leading up to the floor above, and the servants' quarters where they had just searched.

They put the candle on the floor of a cupboard, leaving the door a few inches ajar, so that there was no glare to confuse the eyes, and no shadow to shift about on walls and ceiling. Then they spread the cloak on the floor and sat down to wait, with their backs against the wall.

The moon was now high above the house. Through the open window they could see the comforting stars like friendly eyes watching in the sky. One by one the clocks of the town struck midnight, and when the sounds died away, the deep silence of a windless night fell again over everything. Only the boom of the sea, far away and lugubrious, filled the air with hollow murmurs.

Inside the house the silence became awful; awful, he thought, because any minute now it might be broken by sounds portending terror.

He heard the blood singing in his veins. It sometimes seemed so loud that he fancied it prevented his hearing properly certain other sounds that were beginning very faintly to make themselves audible in the depths of the house. Every time he fastened his attention on these sounds, they instantly ceased. They certainly came no nearer. Yet he could not rid himself of the idea that movement was going on somewhere in the lower regions of the house. The drawing-room floor, where the doors had been so strangely closed, seemed too near; the sounds were farther off than that. He thought of the great kitchen, with the scurrying black beetles, and of the dismal little scullery; but, somehow or other, they did not seem to come from there either.

Then, suddenly, the truth flashed into his mind, and for the space of a minute he felt as if his blood had stopped flowing and turned to ice.

The sounds were not downstairs at all; they were *upstairs* — upstairs, somewhere among those horrid gloomy little servants' rooms with their bits of broken furniture, low ceilings, and cramped windows — upstairs where the victim had first been disturbed and stalked to her death.

And the moment he discovered where the sounds were, he began to hear them more clearly. It was the sound of feet, moving stealthily along the passage overhead, in and out of the rooms, and past the furniture.

He turned quickly to steal a glance at the motionless figure seated beside him, to note whether she had shared his discovery. The faint candlelight coming through the crack in the cupboard door threw her strongly-marked face into vivid relief against the white of the wall.

"Anything wrong?" was all he could think of to say.

"I feel cold—and a little frightened," she whispered.

He offered to close the window, but she seized hold of him and begged him not to leave her side even for an instant.

"It's upstairs, I know," she whispered, with an odd half-laugh, "but I can't possibly go up."

But Shorthouse thought otherwise, knowing that in action lay their best hope of self-control. Every minute he was growing less master of himself, and desperate, aggressive measures were imperative without further delay. Moreover, the action must be taken toward the enemy, not away from it. He could do it now; but in ten minutes he might not have the force left to act for himself, much less for both!

Upstairs, the sounds were becoming louder and closer, accompanied by occasional creaking of the boards. Someone was moving stealthily about, stumbling now and then awkwardly against the furniture. Shorthouse quietly got to his feet, saying in a determined voice:

"Now, Aunt Julia, we'll go upstairs and find out what all this noise is about. You must come too."

He picked up his stick and went to the cupboard for the candle. A limp form rose shakily beside him, breathing hard, and he heard a voice say very faintly something about being "ready to come." The woman's courage amazed him; as they advanced, holding aloft the dripping candle, some subtle force exhaled from this trembling, white-faced old woman at his side that was the true source of his inspiration. It held something really great that shamed him and gave him the support without which he would have proved far less equal to the occasion.

~ ❧ ~

They crossed the dark landing, avoiding with their eyes the deep black space over the banisters. Then they began to mount the narrow staircase to meet the sounds which, minute by minute, grew louder and nearer. About halfway up the stairs Aunt Julia stumbled and Shorthouse turned to catch her by the arm, and just at that moment there came a terrific crash in the servants' corridor overhead. It was instantly followed by a shrill, agonized scream that was a cry of terror and a cry for help melted into one.

Before they could move aside, or go down a single step, someone came rushing along the passage overhead, racing madly, at full speed, three steps at a time, down the very staircase where they stood. The steps were light and uncertain; but close behind them sounded the heavier tread of another person, and the staircase seemed to shake.

Shorthouse and his companion just had time to flatten themselves against the wall when the jumble of flying steps was upon them, and two persons, with the slightest possible interval between them, dashed past at full speed. It was a perfect whirlwind of sound breaking in upon the midnight silence of the empty building.

The two runners, pursuer and pursued, had passed clean through them where they stood, and already with a thud the boards below had received first one, then the other. Yet they had seen absolutely nothing—not a hand, or arm, or face, or even a shred of flying clothing.

There came a second's pause. Then the first one, the lighter of the two, obviously the pursued one, ran with uncertain footsteps into the little room which Shorthouse and his aunt had just left. The heavier one followed. There was a sound of scuffling, gasping, and smothered screaming; and then out onto the landing came the step—of a single person treading weightily.

A dead silence followed for the space of half a minute, and then was heard a rushing sound through the air. It was followed by a dull, crashing thud in the depths of the house below—on the stone floor of the hall.

Utter silence reigned after. Nothing moved. The flame of the candle was steady. It had been steady for the whole time, and the air had been undisturbed by any movement whatsoever. Aunt Julia began fumbling her way downstairs; she was crying gently to herself, and when Shorthouse put his arm around her and half carried her, he felt that she was trembling like a leaf. He went into the little room and picked up the cloak from the floor, and, arm in arm, walking very slowly, without speaking a word or looking once behind them, they marched down the three flights into the hall.

In the hall they saw nothing, but the whole way down the stairs they were conscious that someone followed them; step by step; when they went faster, IT was left behind, and when they went more slowly, IT caught them up. But never once did they look behind to see; and at each turning of the staircase they lowered their eyes for fear of the following horror they might see upon the stairs above.

With trembling hands Shorthouse opened the front door, and they walked out into the moonlight and drew a deep breath of the cool night air blowing in from the sea.

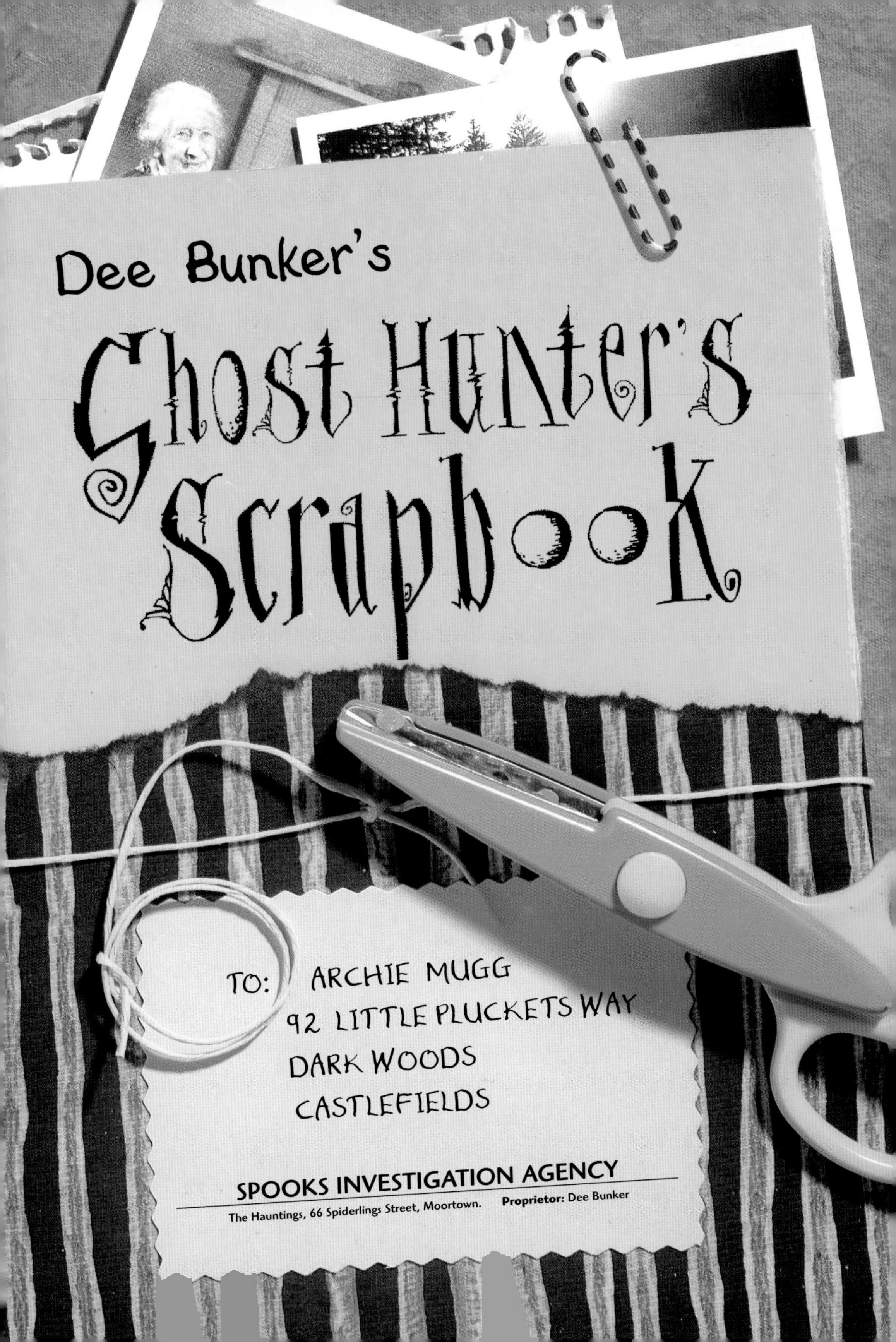

Dee Bunker's

# Ghost Hunter's Scrapbook

TO: ARCHIE MUGG
92 LITTLE PLUCKETS WAY
DARK WOODS
CASTLEFIELDS

**SPOOKS INVESTIGATION AGENCY**

The Hauntings, 66 Spiderlings Street, Moortown.  **Proprietor:** Dee Bunker

# SPOOKS
## INVESTIGATION AGENCY

The Hauntings, 66 Spiderlings Street, Moortown

**Proprietor:** Dee Bunker

Dear Archie

I'm so flattered you want to follow in your great-aunt's footsteps and become a ghost hunter too.

To help you get started, I'm sending along my scrapbook. It's got my notes on all my favorite cases, a few other bits and pieces, and a rather interesting article about yours truly!

One thing I've noticed is that there is more than one kind of ghost. If ever you do find a ghost, look it up in the ghost hunter's field guide I've included. Then you'll know what you're dealing with.

Another thing I've noticed is that ghosts crop up in some places (like graveyards) a lot more than in others. So I've sorted each case by where the haunting takes place and by what type of ghost is involved. You know what a great organizer I am!

Finally, before you start your own investigation, check out my golden rules of ghost hunting, at the back of this scrapbook.

And remember, always tell your parents where you're going. Happy hunting!

Your doting aunt,

Dee
XXX

# KNOW YOUR GHOSTS

Before you go on a ghost hunt, you need to know what you're dealing with. Here's a handy little guide from the Ghost Hunter's Research Center.

## ▶▶▶ GHOSTS AT A GLANCE

**What exactly are ghosts?**
The shades of the deceased which, for one reason or another, still linger among the living.

**What are ghosts made of?**
Possibly pure energy, the same stuff as electricity and radio waves. To study ghosts, study physics and Einstein.

**What do ghosts look like?**
Like people, mostly—as real as the neighbor next door, or more transparent and shadowy. A few are completely invisible but very noisy.

**Are ghosts dangerous?**
Ghosts are scary to the point of goose bumps, but there are almost no cases of their committing murder. Only live people do that.

**Do ghosts ever go naked?** Only when someone has died in the shower.

Most ghosts wear clothes. You can tell a ghost's age by looking at the style of clothing that it's wearing.

**How many ghosts are there?**
Nobody knows. As with icebergs, only the tip of all hauntings gets reported.

ghosts = (pure energy)

Different ghosts behave in different ways. I've stuck in these four pages to help you tell one type from another — like a bird watcher's field guide but written for ghost hunters!

## ▶▶▶ Type: REPLAY GHOSTS

Now and then, if a death involves powerful emotions, a new ghost is created. It lingers on, haunting the place for centuries.

- ➡ **Variations:** Children, adults, animals, even cars, planes, and ships.
- ➡ **Habitat:** Anywhere a person (or animal) dies or is buried in tragic or violent circumstances can become the site of a haunting.
- ➡ **Behavior:** These ghosts act out an event over and over. It might be the details of a crime or an everyday routine.
- ➡ **What to do:** Don't worry, these ghosts haunt places, not people.
- ➡ **Fright factor:** 5/10

### Sighting: ARMY BASE, SOMEWHERE IN ENGLAND, 1944.

Thousands of GIs (American soldiers) stayed in British military bases on their way to the battlefields of World War II.

One night, a GI was in the latrines when another soldier passed by. A moment later he passed the other way. He was in a British uniform and carried an old-fashioned rifle. The GI asked what he was up to, but got no reply. Instead the soldier marched right through him.

The British officers at the base weren't too bothered by this. They knew the latrines were built over the gates of a World War I barracks. A soldier on guard duty there was murdered one night, and for the past 26 years his ghost had kept on patrolling, exactly as his commanding officer had ordered.

## ▶▶▶ Type: REVENGE GHOSTS

These ghosts haunt us with only one thing in mind – getting even.
They're here to sort out unfinished business.

- **Variations:** Some are villains; others are innocent victims.
- **Habitat:** Anywhere there is a person who can receive the ghost's message.
- **Behavior:** Persistent. They never give up.
- **What to do:** Just cooperate.
- **Fright factor:** 9/10

### Sighting: JAPAN, 1700s

About 300 years ago, a farmer called Sogoro
protested to the all-powerful shogun (a warlord)
about the cruel treatment of the peasants by their
local ruler, Kotsuke. Kotsuke was jailed, but
Sogoro was executed for approaching the shogun
without permission. When his ghost came back
to haunt Kotsuke and his wife, Kotsuke begged
for forgiveness and promised to mend his ways.
The hauntings ceased.

## ▶▶▶ Type: CRISIS GHOSTS

Sometimes, the ghost of a LIVING person may drop in on friends
or family just before that person dies or comes close to dying.

- **Variations:** Some bring a message; others visit as if they haven't a care in the world.
- **Habitat:** Anywhere, from the neighbors next door to half the world away.
- **Behavior:** Appear only once. Despite the crisis, they look and act the same as always.
- **What to do:** Nothing. (You may not even realize you've seen a ghost.)
- **Fright factor:** 1/10

### Sighting: See next page.

## Sighting: IRELAND, 1700s

At breakfast one morning, Lady Beresford told her husband she was expecting a letter announcing her darling brother's death. Sure enough, a letter arrived with the sad news.

How did she know? Because her brother's ghost had come to tell her. When she asked it for proof, it laid an icy finger on her wrist, which then withered. For the rest of her life, Lady Beresford wore a black ribbon to hide the injury.

## ▶▶▶ Type: POLTERGEISTS

*Poltergeist* is German for "noisy spirit." These ghosts slam doors, move furniture around, fling things through the air, set fires blazing . . .

- **Variations:** Many, though most poltergeists are invisible and disruptive.
- **Habitat:** Mostly they turn up at people's homes or places of work.
- **Behavior:** Unpredictable. They may come back again and again. Often they focus their energy around one person, especially teenagers and women.
- **What to do:** Duck!
- **Fright factor:** 8/10

## Sighting: TENNESSEE, USA, 1817

John Bell's farm was haunted by a spirit known as the Bell Witch. When future president Andrew Jackson came to stay, he heard the screams of John's daughter Betsy as the spirit pinched and slapped her. Then Jackson's bedding was pulled off and he too was attacked. Oddly, the spirit was kind to Mrs. Bell. It even sang to her.

In 1820, John Bell fell violently ill and died. As if its work was done, the spirit left.

# ▶▶▶ Type: ANIMAL GHOSTS

Phantom pets often come back to visit former homes and owners.

- ⊡ **Variations:** Cats and dogs are more common than goldfish and guinea pigs.
- ⊡ **Habitat:** Around their former homes.
- ⊡ **Behavior:** Usually friendly.
- ⊡ **Fright factor:** 4/10

## Sighting: AUSTRALIA, 1953

William Courtney was heartbroken when Lady, his greyhound, died. The next night, lying in bed in the dark, he heard a dog patter into his room and flop down on the floor beside him – just like Lady used to. When he turned on the light, the room was empty. Lady's ghost was gone.

# ▶▶▶ Type: PHANTOM TRAFFIC

The tragedy of death seems to turn vehicles as well as people into ghosts.

- ⊡ **Variations:** Sometimes just the lights are seen; sometimes the whole machine.
- ⊡ **Habitat:** The same routes that were originally traveled.
- ⊡ **Behavior:** Obeys the rules of the road.
- ⊡ **Fright factor:** 4/10

## Sighting: ILLINOIS, USA, 1866–present

President Abraham Lincoln was shot on April 14, 1865. A funeral train took his body home from Washington to Illinois. Ever since, on the anniversary of that journey, people have reported a phantom train on that same stretch of track. The steam engine belches smoke but makes no sound. The carriages are draped with black flags.

# Meet a Real-life Ghost Hunter

*Fame at last! Not a good photo of me, though.*

**Dee Bunker travels the world in pursuit of ghosts. We tracked her down at her home, headquarters of the famous *Spooks Investigation Agency,* and asked her some searching questions.**

*A quiet night in is rare for investigator Dee Bunker*

**How do you start?** "First I choose a ghost. New ghosts are hard to find. It's easier to investigate the ghosts that other people have already reported. Newspapers, magazines, and the Internet are full of the latest sightings."

**What's the key to success?** "Be prepared. Ghosts are elusive, so I have to be thorough. First I find out all I can about a case and what type of ghost is involved. That way I know what to look for.

Then I arrange permission to visit the site of the haunting (I never trespass) and meet any witnesses.

Before setting out, I test all my equipment. A dead battery is no problem at home. It's murder when you're in a haunted house without a working flashlight."

# Oh, no! I forgot my . . .

**The one thing that drives Dee Bunker nuts when she's on a ghost hunt is not having the right equipment. So she keeps a ready-packed shoulder bag on a hook by the front door.**

**1.** Flashlight.

**2.** Camera with flash to record details of a site. (Or paper and pencil to make sketches.)

**3.** Dictaphone to record any observations. (Or paper and pencil to write them down.)

**4.** Digital thermometer to measure sudden changes in the temperature. Ghosts and cold spots go together.

**5.** Image intensifier to see things in the dark. It's 100 times better than the naked eye.

**6.** Camcorder to record live action and sound.

*plus (not numbered above)*

**7.** Glow-in-the-dark watch to keep track of the time.

**8.** Stick of chalk to mark the position of objects in case they move or are moved.

**9.** Talcum powder to dust the floor. Ghosts don't leave tracks, people do.

**10.** Masking tape to seal doors and windows. Ghosts can find other ways into a room, people can't.

**11.** Cotton thread to booby-trap doorways and halls. Only a living body will snap it.

**12.** Spare batteries for flashlight.

# Dee Bunker asks: What was that?

## SPOOKY HAPPENINGS . . .

## OR NATURAL CAUSES?

| SPOOKY HAPPENINGS . . . | OR NATURAL CAUSES? |
| --- | --- |
| Repeated knockings | Central heating pipes are acting up |
| Creaking footsteps | Old floorboards contracting as the temperature drops |
| Spooky cold spots | Drafts or holes near walls and windows |
| Ghostly lights on the ceiling | Reflections from road traffic |
| A scratching poltergeist | Birds on roof, or mice in walls or ceilings |
| A shadowy figure on a wall | A damp patch |
| Pale phantoms on the road | Wispy fog |
| Ghostly lights in the woods | Moonbeams |

### What do you look for?

"Rational explanations, not ghosts! That sounds odd, doesn't it? But you can't let your imagination run wild."

### Have you ever found a ghost?

"Not yet. I've been hunting ghosts since I was a child, and I can't give up now. It's the looking, not the finding, that's fun."

# "It's the looking, not the finding, that's fun"

### Do you believe in ghosts?

"That's a tough question. Most scientists say there is no proof that ghosts exist. Others say there is no proof that they don't exist. I'm inclined to agree with the scientists. What do you think?"

### What else do you look for?

"Witnesses, if possible, though they're hard to find. You see, ghost stories spread like wildfire. With every retelling they get less accurate. But eyewitnesses get muddled too. So I ask them to write down what they saw and heard. And I double-check what they tell me with other people."

### What do you do with the information?

"I file it. Each case gets its own file. That's where I keep all the records of what has taken place: witness statements, photos, maps, newspaper cuttings— everything."

▷ *Dee finds stories to investigate from many sources—newspapers and the Internet are her favorites.*

GHOST SH

The *Lady Luvibund* is missing — has anyone seen this ship?

On February 13, 1748, the three-masted *Lady Luvibund* sailed into a sandbank and sank with the loss of all hands. Jealousy over the captain's wife had driven the first mate to commit murder and sabotage the ship's steering.

*Come Camping! Magazine*

*English redcoats defeated*

## There
our

● ONE DARK NOVEMBEM in 1956, two students cam Cuillin Hills on the Isle of woken by strange noises. out of their tent and saw warriors in kilts charging hillside. The air felt strangely even for Scotland.

The next night the same the two campers. The same the air. This time, though,

This case started with a newspaper clipping sent by a cousin in Australia, way back in 1955.

# STONE ME

### *It's raining rocks!*

**L**AST WEEK while Western Australia prayed for rain for the crops, the Smith family near Mount Barker prayed for the rain to stop. Why? Because over at their farmhouse it's been raining rocks, not water!

Gilbert and Jean Smith have been holed up in their house for several days and nights while pebbles from gravel-size to egg-size pelted down on them. Some of the pebbles have landed inside the house, even though there are no holes in the roof. Strangely, no one has been hit. When the Smiths started to pick up the stones, a lot of them felt warm to red-hot.

**Now other farmhouses are looking out for heavy showers.**

A local mystic came by to investigate earlier this week. He thinks the showers of stones might be linked to Mrs. Smith's dad, who was critically ill.

Yesterday we learned that Mrs. Smith's father has passed away, and that the showers have stopped.

I was stone broke in those days, so it took a few years to save up for the airfare to Perth.

## CASE NOTES

9:00 A.M.   I rent a Jeep at the airport. Boy, is it hot out here!

2:00 P.M.   250 miles and one flat tire later, I arrive at the Smiths' farmhouse. It looks deserted.

TORNADOES WHIRL ALONG AT UP TO 300 MILES PER HOUR. DID ONE PASS BY THE SMITHS'?

2:10 P.M.   Inside, my digital thermometer reads 95F—so no spooky cold spots here.

2:25 P.M.   Eureka, a pebble in the kitchen! I take it with me for analysis.

3:00 P.M.   Visit the town paper. The editor says no reporter ever saw the pebbles.

3:45 P.M.   I drop in on the local weather station to ask about freak showers. Waterspouts and tornadoes sometimes sweep up sand, hay, even frogs, and then drop them miles away.

5:00 P.M.   Must go. Cousin Sandy is expecting me for a barbie.

CONCLUSION: The case is so old that the trail's gone cold. Was it a poltergeist or was it the weather? No clues from my pebble—it's just a pebble. Case unsolved.

**COME CAMPING!** *Magazine*

*English redcoats defeated Highland rebels in 1746. Have the rebels returned?*

# There Are Ghosts on our Campsite!

● ONE DARK NOVEMBER night back in 1956, two students camping in the Cuillin Hills on the Isle of Skye were woken by strange noises. They looked out of their tent and saw Highland warriors in kilts charging across the hillside. The air felt strangely clammy, even for Scotland.

The next night the same noises woke the two campers. The same chill hung in the air. This time, though, the band of Highland warriors stumbled along as if worn out by exhaustion and defeat.

Locals reckon the ghostly army might be part of the Jacobite rebellion led by Charles Edward Stuart against the English Crown in 1745. When the rebellion failed, Bonnie Prince Charlie fled for his life – over the sea to the Isle of Skye.

So, if you happen to go camping in the Cuillin Hills, keep your eyes peeled!

★

To investigate this story, I had to go camping – in November too! I flew to Glasgow, had tea with my cousins the McBunkers, and caught the ferry to Skye.

## CASE NOTES

**6:00 P.M.** Park my rented car (a Rolls Royce Silver Ghost) close to the students' campsite.

**8:00 P.M.** Night falls. Wrap myself in a tartan rug and pour a wee dram of whiskey to keep warm.

**MIDNIGHT** Is that the wind howling, or bagpipes wailing? I suddenly feel cold and hang my digital thermometer out of the car window. By flashlight I watch the temperature plunge to -20°F.

**12:15 A.M.** Are those people I see through the swirling mist? Nothing shows up on my night-vision image intensifier.

**12:30–5:30 A.M.** Sleep fitfully, dreaming, waking, and dreaming again. It's hard to separate fact from fantasy.

**6:00 A.M.** Pack up and leave. No sign of ghostly soldiers, but what a thrilling camping trip!

Wonderful heather up here!

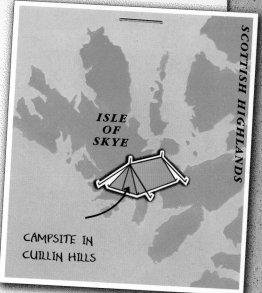

SCOTTISH HIGHLANDS

ISLE OF SKYE

CAMPSITE IN CUILLIN HILLS

**CONCLUSION:** Two witnesses and a local tradition of ghost soldiers don't prove anything. Not when freezing fog creates strange shapes and the wind howls all night long. Case closed.

CATEGORY: Graveyards/Replay Ghosts
SIGHTING: Chicago, USA, 1991

# GHOST IN CEMETERY

**DO YOU KNOW THIS WOMAN?** Chicago's own Ghost Research Society thinks she's a ghost. A G.R.S. member photographed her in one of America's most haunted sites: Bachelor's Grove Cemetery.

*The Ghost Research Society*

**The Ghost Research Society photo that may prove the existence of ghosts.**

Situated in a spooky wood on the edge of town, Bachelor's Grove has been a graveyard since 1864. Over the years people claim to have spotted glowing lights, phantom cars, and over 100 ghosts.

The Ghost Research Society investigated the cemetery on August 10 and saw a young woman dressed in old-fashioned clothes and perched on a tomb-stone. She seemed to be almost transparent, but a camera caught her image pretty clearly.

When the photo was first developed, it caused a sensation. We are printing a copy here for our readers to make up their own minds.

Most people dread graveyards, but ghost hunters love them! As soon as I saw the Ghost Research Society photo in my local newspaper, I got on the phone to book a seat on the next flight to Chicago.

## CASE NOTES:

1:00 P.M.  I arrive in Chicago, but my ghost hunting kit has gone to Chile. Bad start.

2:00 P.M.  Take a cab to the cemetery. Although it was abandoned in the '60s, I notice fresh tire tracks on the lane through the woods. The place is a real dump, with gravestones covered in graffiti and litter. No kit, so no point hanging around.

4:30 P.M.  Visit the local police station. The desk sergeant says the cemetery is popular with vandals and joy riders. They might be mistaken for "ghosts," their stolen vehicles for "phantom" cars... (Coffee and doughnut in the cafeteria—yum!)

7:00 P.M.  Driving past the cemetery again, I see hoodlums around a bonfire. The sparks might set other garbage alight, and might account for stories of glowing lights.

7:45 P.M.  Check in to my hotel—glad to be in a comfy bed and not the cemetery.

CONCLUSION: The sightings are typical of many graveyards and seem easily explained. But I don't have a clue about the woman in the photo—must contact the Ghost Research Society. Case still under investigation.

STATION CAFE

23359      334

BLACK COFFEE  50c
DOUGHNUT  $1.25

10/2/91   04:55

# The Haunted Café

*from our restaurant critic*

**S**TARTLING NEWS from Georgetown, Colorado. Employees at the *FULL CIRCLE CAFÉ* report wailing, smashed dishes, flying dishcloths, and falling photos. Not to mention a transparent man in old-fashioned clothes!

**I**n **1867** a Scot called Bainbridge lost at a game of cards and shot his opponent. A group of outraged citizens hanged Bainbridge without trial. Before he died, he cursed the crowd and swore he'd haunt them and all their descendants.

Sure enough, a poltergeist turned up the following year, at the house where Bainbridge had been locked up. The angry ghost slammed doors and blew out lanterns.

### STILL HANGING AROUND

Twenty years later, an apparition of a man with a knotted rope around his neck terrified a girl not far from the exact spot where Bainbridge was hanged.

Now he's back! But why the café? Is he hungry?

*Poker games were never peaceful.*

Bainbridge swore revenge. Could someone at the café be related to the people he cursed?

None of my ancestors lived in Georgetown, so I was safe from the Bainbridge curse. I flew to Denver, took a Greyhound bus to Georgetown, and arrived in time for lunch at the café.

## CASE NOTES:

2:45 P.M. Interview the waitress. But she's new and hasn't seen anything unusual.

3:00 P.M. Ditto the cook. He heard the story from the last cook, who's left town.

3:30 P.M. The town library has old newspaper reports about the hanging, but no firsthand accounts. Survey maps are more helpful.
They show abandoned silver mines in the area. Rockfalls could cause falling dishes and pictures. Groaning timber shafts might sound like human wailing.

Above: Timber shafts in a 19th-century silver mine

FULL CIRCLE CAFÉ
WAFFLES $1.20
BACON 50¢
O. JUICE $2.50

TOTAL: $4.20

HAVE A NICE DAY!

7/3/96   08:40

8:00 P.M. Dinner at the Full Circle. After closing time, I set up surveillance. Dust the floors with talc (ghosts don't leave footprints; humans do), booby-trap all exits with thread, switch on my camcorder, and retire to my hotel.

8:30 A.M. Breakfast at the Full Circle. No signs of entry. Nothing on the camcorder.

CONCLUSION: Nice town, nice story, but my money's on the mines, not Bainbridge. Case closed.

CATEGORY: Golf Courses/Replay Ghosts
SIGHTING: Canada, 1997

 Golf Magazine

**HOLE 1**

**HOLE 2**

# Spooky!

**A**BOUT 100 years ago at Fort MacLeod, Alberta, two liquor smugglers took a short walk. This was no Sunday stroll. They had handcuffs on their wrists and an armed escort at their side.

After they trudged up the gallows steps, a Canadian Mountie placed a thick noose around each neck. Moments later it was over. Law on the frontier was harsh and swift.

Fast forward to the present and the fort has gone. Now there's a golf course here. Where the two smugglers were hanged is the tee-off for the second hole. Their bodies lie buried somewhere under the fairway to the first hole.

It all looks nice and peaceful—except that, from time to time, at sunrise, employees maintaining the course claim to see two figures dangling eerily in mid-air on the tee-off for the second hole.

Golf and ghosts are my two great passions. So when I saw this magazine article I just had to fly to Canada.

40

## CASE NOTES

**2:00 P.M.** I arrive in Calgary, Alberta. So does my ghost hunter's kit. My golf bag has gone to Calcutta.

**5:30 P.M.** Take a cab from my hotel to the golf course. Arrive in time for cocktails in the clubhouse. Hear a lot of tall stories, and rent clubs for a round of golf tomorrow.

**6:00 A.M.** Tee off at the first hole. The early morning light filters through the trees and casts strange shadows.

**6:15 A.M.** Tee off at the second hole. Darn these shadows. I miss the ball completely...

**6:20 A.M.** Give up golf and set up my digital thermometer (in case of a ghostly drop in the temperature) and my new, portable infrared detector (to detect the body heat of anyone posing as a ghost). Nothing at the second hole.
Ditto the first hole.

**8:00 A.M.** Breakfast at the clubhouse.

**10:00 A.M.** Visit the local museum. Great model fort and old uniforms, but no record of smugglers and hangings.

ADMIT ONE

THE MUSEUM OF CANADIAN THINGS

THESE TWO FIGURES ARE GOLFERS, NOT GHOSTS. HOPE THEY DIDN'T SEE MY TERRIBLE PUTT!

## CONCLUSION:
People are more likely to see ghosts if they already expect to see them. So if one story gets out, it often triggers others. Anyway, golfers always exaggerate. Case closed.

**FEBRUARY 12, 1998**

# GHOST SHIP LOST

The *Lady Luvibund* is missing – has anyone seen this ship?

**On February 13, 1748, the three-masted *Lady Luvibund* sailed into a sandbank and sank with the loss of all hands. Jealousy over the captain's wife had driven the first mate to commit murder and sabotage the ship's steering.**

Fifty years later, the captain of a trading vessel saw a three-master bear down on him, and just managed to swing away in time. Fishermen nearby also saw the three-master run into a sandbank and break up. Oddly, though, they couldn't find any wreckage. Then, in 1848, local seamen rushed out in lifeboats to rescue a ship they saw founder in the same place. Again, no wreckage. Fifty years later, in 1898, there was a third wave of sightings.

That explains why, on February 13, 1948, ghost hunters set out from Ramsgate to search for the ship that appears every 50 years. Sadly, it failed to show up. Will it this time?

When I read in my paper that the *Lady Luvibund* was due
to appear the very next day, I nearly choked on my toast.
At last I would see a ghost, even if it was only an old wreck.

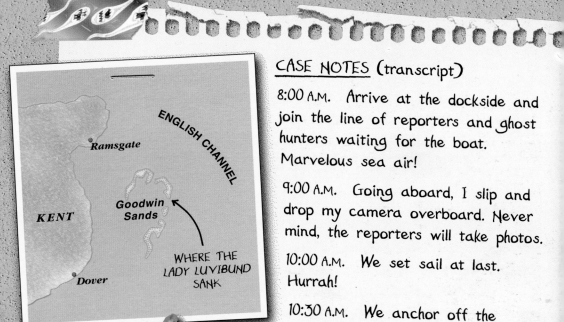

KENT

Ramsgate

Dover

ENGLISH CHANNEL

Goodwin Sands

WHERE THE
LADY LUVIBUND
SANK

## CASE NOTES (transcript)

8:00 A.M.  Arrive at the dockside and join the line of reporters and ghost hunters waiting for the boat. Marvelous sea air!

9:00 A.M.  Going aboard, I slip and drop my camera overboard. Never mind, the reporters will take photos.

10:00 A.M.  We set sail at last. Hurrah!

10:30 A.M.  We anchor off the sandbank where the *Lady Luvibund* sank. Hope the wind drops soon. It's too rough for writing notes—luckily I have my dictaphone.

1:00 P.M.  Nothing yet. Feeling a little sick, so I feed my sandwiches to the gulls.

4:30 P.M.  Ashore again. No *Lady Luvibund*, but there's always plenty of other ghosts in the sea to catch.

CONCLUSION: Whether the *Lady Luvibund* really did haunt that sandbank, or just the vivid imaginations of local sailors, we shall probably never know. Case pending till 2048—too late for your old aunt, but not for you, Archie!

## THE CASE OF THE PHANTOM MOTORCYCLIST

"One hot summer night, two boys called Tony and Dave were fishing at a pond by some old railroad tracks. Close to 10:00 P.M. they set out for home.

At the railroad crossing they heard the roar of a motorcycle going flat out. A moment later they saw a shape crouched low over the handlebars of a big bike. It was heading straight for where they stood. They dropped their rods and dived for cover. The bike hit the crossing, sailed over the tracks, and crashed into a ditch.

The boys ran off to get help. When the police and ambulance arrived, they found the boys' fishing gear but no trace of the motorbike or rider. Not a drop of oil was spilled; not a blade of grass was crushed.

By this time, some local people had turned up to see what all the fuss was about. One old lady said she remembered a reckless young motorcyclist who'd played 'chicken' here—he'd race trains to the crossing to see if he could get over first. One night he lost the race, and his life. Ever since, people have seen the ghostly rider and his bike go racing by again."

Archie, this story shows you should NEVER play around on the railroad tracks. It also shows that some investigations stop before they start.

# WANTED
## Witnesses for Accident

Do you know two friends called Tony and Dave? They may have vital information about a crash involving a phantom motorbike. They are both keen fishermen. If you can help,

### contact Dee Bunker
**c/o FISHING WEEKLY**
**P.O. Box 876**

I heard this story from the station master, while waiting for a train, and jotted it down on the back of an envelope. He'd heard it from someone else. He didn't know when or where the haunting took place, or who the two boys were.

I tried to find the boys by putting a notice in fishing magazines and the local newspaper. I also looked for the story in the library and on the Internet. Alas, in vain.

So, was there a phantom bike? Or did the boys already know about the motorcyclist and invent his ghost as a joke, or as an excuse for coming home late?

CONCLUSION: Case abandoned.

# SPOOKS
## INVESTIGATION AGENCY

The Hauntings, 66 Spiderlings Street, Moortown

**Proprietor: Dee Bunker**

## DEE BUNKER'S GOLDEN RULES OF GHOST HUNTING

1. Always tell your family where you're going.

2. Play safe and take a friend-you'll have an extra pair of eyes and ears, and more fun.

3. Take a snack-but don't leave litter.

4. Never, never trespass.

5. Look for rational explanations, not ghosts.

6. If you see or hear a ghost, stay calm-or panic very quietly.

7. Start to gather evidence, without scaring the ghost away.

8. If you have a camera or camcorder, shoot pictures for all you're worth. Otherwise sketch what you see.

9. Make notes of everything that happens while it's fresh in your mind. This includes size, shape, color, smell, solid or transparent, walking or floating, temperature change, time, weather, location.

SIR GHASTLIE MONES 1503-?
(MUSEUM FOUNDER)

THE NATIONAL MUSEUM
— OF —
PHONY GHOSTS

SOUVENIR GUIDE

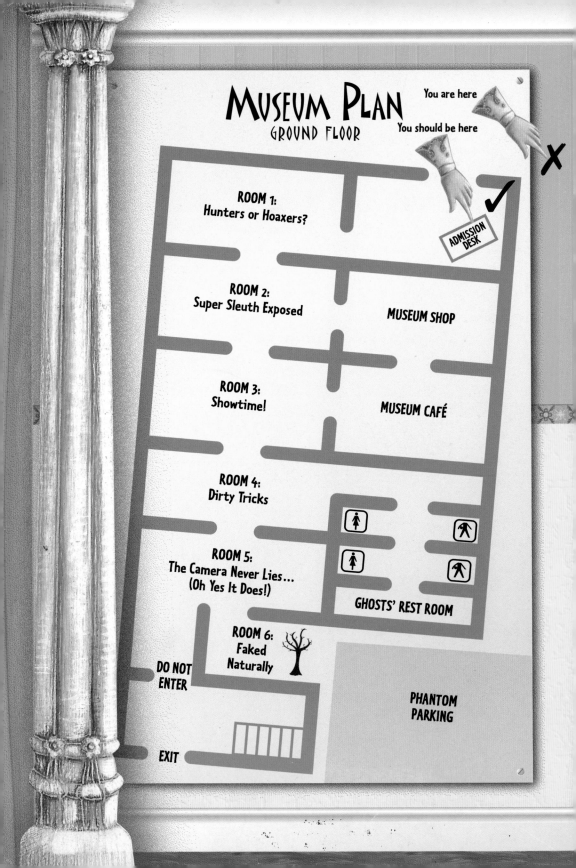

# WELCOME TO MY WORLD-FAMOUS COLLECTION OF BOGUS GHOSTS AND PHONY PHANTOMS.

**A**S YOU WILL SEE, not a single one is really real, or even half true. All the spooks on display here are the work of crafty scoundrels who set out to pull the wool over the eyes of an innocent public.

These ridiculous fakes did dreadful damage to the reputation of real ghosts. No one took us seriously. I know, because I am one. Don't worry, I'm harmless. I just want to expose the rogues who are responsible. To see the exhibits,

## STEP THIS WAY,

and discover the truth for yourself!

(The National Museum of Phony Ghosts has 273 rooms. Most are open only to ghosts who come here for purposes of research, but a small number of rooms are open to the public. Just follow the signs.)

### ENTRANCE

• EXHIBIT 1 •
1. A SCENE FROM THE MOVIE OF THE AMITYVILLE HORROR

WE ♥ AMITYVILLE

## ROOM 1

# HUNTERS OR HOAXERS?

IF YOU ASK ME, ghost hunting and ghost hoaxing are two sides of the same coin. Either the hunters bamboozle you with fakes or someone else bamboozles them!

**Exhibit 1: The Amityville Horror, 1974**
Number 112 Ocean Avenue was a quiet house in a quiet town called Amityville, New York—until 23-year-old Ronnie DeFeo picked up a gun on November 13,

1974, and shot his entire family.

One year later the Lutz family moved in. After just 28 days, they emerged with spine-tingling reports of putrid smells, stairs dripping with green slime, an attic swarming with billions of flies, a secret room painted blood red, phantom marching bands, poltergeists, even a demon pig.

These reports quickly turned into a book and then a movie. Both were smash hits. But investigators smelled

OINK

• EXHIBIT 2 •

2B. LONG WHITE BEARD
(100% WOOL)

2C. CLANKING CHAINS

2A. KING LOUIS IX

NO KEY

BZZZZZZ

a rat, and most people now accept it was a hoax. All the Lutz family proved was that a well-planned haunting gets great publicity.

**Exhibit 2: The Haunted Palace, 1259**
King Louis IX of France once gave six monks a big house at Chantilly, not far from Paris. But the ungrateful monks had their eye on the royal palace of Vauvert nearby. Strange goings-on began to be reported there.

Clanking chains and unearthly shrieks echoed along the corridors. And a roving phantom with a long white beard, a green robe, and a serpent's tail made a good night's sleep impossible.

The monks volunteered to get rid of the ghosts, provided everyone else moved out. As soon as the monks had the palace to themselves the hauntings stopped. Is this proof of (1) the power of prayer or (2) a cunning plan? My bets are on number two.

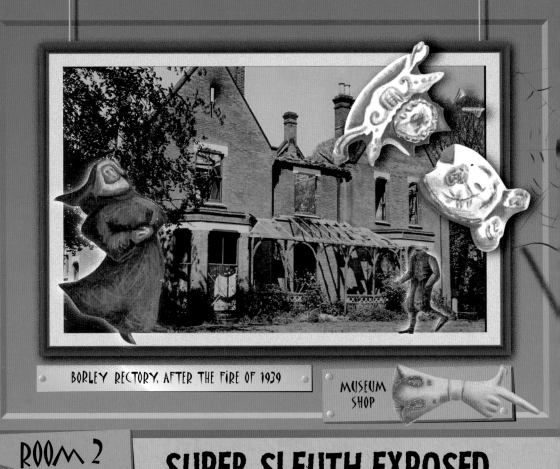

BORLEY RECTORY, AFTER THE FIRE OF 1939

MUSEUM SHOP

# SUPER SLEUTH EXPOSED

HARRY PRICE was the world's greatest ghost hunter—or so he said. His favorite case was Borley Rectory, a rambling Victorian house in Essex, England.

Locals claimed the house stood on the site of an old monastery. It didn't, but visitors were thrilled by tales of a ghostly nun, a headless man, and a phantom coach. In 1929 Harry Price was asked to investigate. As soon as he arrived, bells in the servants' quarters began to ring, a vase smashed itself, and spooky footsteps echoed through the hall. The minister living there had soon had enough and left.

The new tenants, the Reverend Foyster and his wife, Marianne, seemed to drive the house wild. Keys flew out of locks, furniture fell over, and messages were scribbled on the walls. The tormented couple put up with this for five years—then they moved out too.

DING! DING!

THE PHANTOM COACH

THE KEY THAT FLEW OUT OF A LOCK AND THE VASE THAT SMASHED ITSELF

HARRY PRICE (LEFT) WITH THE FOYSTER FAMILY IN 1931

Next Harry rented the place and put in a team of 48 volunteer investigators. They found some odd lights and noises, but nothing very convincing.

In 1939 Borley Rectory burned down, and Harry's decade of ghost hunting there came to an end.

In 1948, at age 67, Harry died. Big mistake! Other researchers re-examined his evidence and came to some startling conclusions:

## BORLEY BUNGLES

● **Cover-ups!** Rats gnawing on wires made bells ring, but Harry ignored these and other natural causes.

● **Unreliable evidence!** Many of the ghostly sightings were reported only by Marianne Foyster. Years later she admitted she'd faked some of them.

● **Shoddy methods!** Harry's team of amateurs was told to look for ghosts. They should have been told to look for rational explanations.

● **Hype!** Harry exaggerated his findings to win publicity and fame. It worked.

This leaves just one real mystery: why people still think the Rectory was haunted and Harry Price was a good ghost hunter.

LEAH FOX, C. 1817-1891

KATIE FOX, C. 1836-1892

MAGGIE FOX, C. 1833-1893

# SHOWTIME!

THE FOX SISTERS, Catherine (12) and Margaretta (15), were fooling around in their room when they hit upon a fun way to hold a conversation with the ghost that was supposed to haunt their house. The year was 1848. The place was Hydesville, New York.

First their mother was invited to listen in, then the neighbors.

The girls asked the ghost to knock once if the answer to a question was "yes" and twice if "no." It was a simple code. Any ghost could follow it.

Katie, Maggie, and the ghost soon got chatting, and the ghost revealed that he'd been murdered by a previous resident and buried in the cellar.

Katie and Maggie took their show on the road, with their older sister

CLAP        CLAP

**KNOCK KNOCK! WHOOOOOOO'S THERE?**

PHALANGES HOMO SAPIENS

TOE JOINTS, POSSIBLY KATIE'S

THE FOX SHOW, 1850

CAFÉ

Leah as manager. Ghost talking spread like measles all across America. Soon hundreds of people claimed they could do it.

After seven years of fame, the Fox sisters had an attack of guilt. They announced the whole show was faked. The knocking noise of the ghost was really the cracking of their toe joints.

But talking to ghosts was so thrilling that people refused to believe the girls' confession. They forced them to take it back. Not until Maggie was an old woman did she find the courage to show an audience how simple the trick was.

Did Maggie's confession drive a nail into the coffin of spirit rapping? No, people still pay to go to séances and talk to ghosts. Not that the ghosts ever see any of the money!

CLAP                    CLAP

## • EXHIBIT 1 •

## • EXHIBIT 2 •

1. THE VEST THAT GAVE IT AWAY

2A. HARRY HOUDINI, 1874-1926

2B. HOUDINI'S
LOCKS AND CHAINS

## ROOM 4

# DIRTY TRICKS

IN THE 1850s, certain charlatans began to call themselves mediums. They claimed they used special powers to contact the ghosts of loved ones—for a fee. In fact, they used conjuring tricks and mumbo jumbo.

## Exhibit 1. That's Torn It

One medium swore the strange ripping noises at her sessions were made by the unhappy spirit of a young girl. Someone switched on the lights mid-

act and caught the medium stuffing a half-torn vest under her dress.

That's not all! Tables were rocked, not by ghosts, but by mediums sliding a foot under one leg. And doors were opened by tugging on rigged-up string. No wonder they dimmed the lights.

## Exhibit 2. Knot Fair

Houdini was a famous magician and escape artist who could wriggle out of all kinds of locks and chains. He knew

• EXHIBIT 3 •

3A.—3C. ECTOPLASM GALORE

every trick in the book, and he loved to expose cheats.

Margery, an American medium, claimed she could summon ghosts with the help of her dead brother, Walter. The day Houdini locked her in a wooden box, she couldn't summon a single ghost.

## Exhibit 3. Star Attraction

Ectoplasm, yuk! By the early 1900s, this stuff was pouring out of mediums—out of their mouth, nose, ears, navel, everywhere. They said it was an astral substance which helped them call up and give shape to ghosts. Scientists said it was usually a mixture of soap, gelatin, and egg-white. Or chewed-up paper. Or, for the really impressive results shown here, sheets of a fine gauzy material called muslin.

SPIRIT PHOTOS TAKEN BY R. CHILD BAYLEY, 1910 (ABOVE)
AND EDOUARD BUGUET, 1873 (BELOW)

1. PRESIDENT LINCOLN'S WIDOW

2. PRESIDENT LINCOLN

3. LINCOLN'S WIDOW WITH THE "GHOST" OF HER LATE HUSBAND

## ROOM 5 | THE CAMERA NEVER LIES...

IN 1861, WHEN photography was still a new science, William Mumler of Boston photographed himself twice by mistake on the same piece of film. When he printed the photo, both images showed up. He had stumbled on the joys of double exposure—which means taking a second photograph on the same piece of film as the first.

Mumler at once spotted a shady way to make money. He began to take portrait photos of wealthy people and used double exposure to add a "spirit," usually of someone who was near and dear to them. The ghostly figure might hover over one shoulder, as if it were keeping a kind and watchful eye on the sitter. These "spirits," however, were all borrowed from other photos.

Mumler's greatest coup was to persuade President Lincoln's widow to sit for him. His pictures of her and the ghost of Old Abe fooled everyone— until Mumler was exposed as a fake.

1. GRANNY'S GHOST?
NO, A VORTEX

2. A GRAVEYARD GHOST?
NO, A MIST

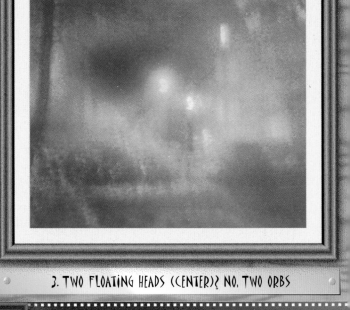

3. TWO FLOATING HEADS (CENTER)? NO, TWO ORBS

**M**ODERN GHOST PHOTOS aren't any better than Mumler's. Most of them fall into three categories:

**1. VORTEXES** are white clouds shaped like a tornado. They're caused by a wisp of hair in front of the camera lens, or a flash reflected off the camera strap.

**2. MISTS** are foggy white patches in front of or behind other objects in the photo. They appear when a hairline crack in the camera case lets in light.

**3. ORBS** are small, pale globes of light that look very ghostly. In fact they are water spots or flaws on the film.

# FAKED NATURALLY

**T**AKE CITY PEOPLE into the countryside, and the screech of an owl turns them to jelly. Here we show Mother Nature as the greatest hoaxer of them all.

Have you ever glimpsed small lights flickering in the woods? People once thought these were spirits luring travelers off the road, or headless ghosts carrying lanterns as they looked for missing heads.

These will-o'-the-wisps and jack-o'-lanterns are actually marsh gas, made by rotting vegetation. The flames dance in the breeze as if they have a mind of their own. They are invisible in bright sunlight, which is why you see them only at night.

EXIT

# SPECIAL OFFERS

YOUR CHANCE TO MEET REAL GHOSTS.

GHOST RIDE TAKE A SEAT ON OUR DUNGEON EXPRESS. NIGHTMARES GUARANTEED!

FANCY DRESS A COSTUME PARTY FOR THE BRAVE. SEE IF YOU CAN TELL THE GUESTS FROM THE REAL GHOSTS WHO WORK HERE.

MIDNIGHT FEAST STAY BEHIND AS WE LOCK THE DOORS FOR THE SLUMBER PARTY WHERE NO ONE SLEEPS!

## ROOMS 8-273
KEEP OUT

# BYE...

**W**ELL DONE, you've reached the end of the tour. If my museum makes you wary of scallywags who say they have seen a ghost or can contact one, then it has done a good job.

# MICHAEL JOHNSTONE  MOVIE MOGUL

Palm Tree Boulevard, Hollywood, CA 34500

Chris,

Come and check out my local movie theater—it specializes in ghost movies, and I think it may be haunted. (There's never a line for tickets, yet every show is packed with Hollywood stars I thought were long gone.) Here's the program for what's on. See you next Friday!

Michael

## MOVIE RATINGS

| | |
|---|---|
| Suitable for all | G |
| Parental Guidance—some scenes unsuitable for young children | PG |
| Suitable for those ages 13 and over | PG-13 |
| Restricted—those under 17 not admitted without parent or guardian | R |

## RATINGS GUIDE

| | |
|---|---|
| FLICKER OF INTEREST | ☠ |
| YOU'LL STAY AWAKE | ☠☠ |
| PRETTY GOOD | ☠☠☠ |
| REALLY GREAT | ☠☠☠☠ |
| TO DIE FOR—DON'T MISS IT | ☠☠☠☠☠ |

## NIGHTMARE ZONE

Some of the best-known ghost movies are also some of the goriest—NIGHTMARE ON ELM STREET, THE AMITYVILLE HORROR, and the like. And because they are Rated R, we have decided not to include them.

# FRIDAY NIGHT IS FRIGHT NIGHT!

Megascreens for megascreams. Refreshments available during intermission.

## SCREEN ONE

### SILENT AS THE GRAVE
Phantoms from the first flicks

## SCREEN TWO

### GHOSTLY GIGGLES
Amusing apparitions and hysterical hauntings

## SCREEN THREE

### GHOSTS ON THE RAMPAGE
Murder and mayhem—bring a friend!

## SCREEN FOUR

### GHOSTS IN LOVE
Moving moments for the misty-eyed

## SCREEN FIVE

### CLASSICAL GHOSTS
Specters from Shakespeare, Dickens, and Wilde

## SCREEN SIX

### MUSICAL GHOSTS
Singing spirits and spinning specters

## SCREEN SEVEN

### SOB STORY
For baseball fans, a tearjerker with a happy ending

# SILENT AS THE GRAVE

**T**here were no voices to listen to in early films, which is why we call them silent movies. Although the first movie ghosts were silent, the audiences weren't. Their screams of terror rang through the picture palaces.

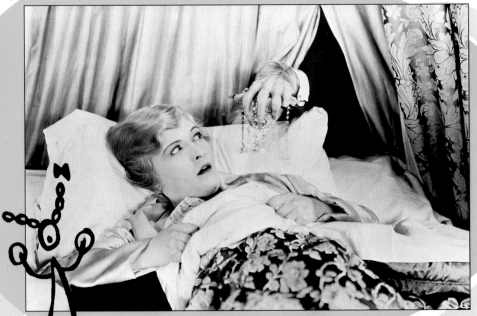

He's behind you! A menacing moment from
**THE CAT AND THE CANARY.**

*7:00 P.M.* Fright Night starts with **THE CAT AND THE CANARY** (1927). This silent classic is the forerunner of many a movie featuring a haunted house and the nervous guests who are forced to spend a night in it.

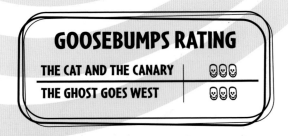

## GOOSEBUMPS RATING

| | |
|---|---|
| THE CAT AND THE CANARY | 😃😃😃 |
| THE GHOST GOES WEST | 😃😃😃 |

Because silent movies had no sound, captions appeared on the screen every few minutes for audiences to read what had just been said. And atmospheric music was provided by the movie theater's own piano or organ.

**9:00 P.M.** When sound arrived, **THE CAT AND THE CANARY** (1939) was remade as a "talkie" with wise-cracking Bob Hope, gorgeous Paulette Goddard, and lots of spooky sound effects. It was a big hit.

Corny but creepy, and about to pounce in
THE CAT AND THE CANARY.

**STAR CHOICE**

**11:00 P.M.** **THE GHOST GOES WEST** (1936) is another "talkie." It tells the tale of an American millionaire who ships a Scottish castle to his Florida estate—lock, stock, and ghost. Screen idol Robert Donat stars in the dual role as the spirit who spooks everyone there is to spook, and as his bankrupt descendant who is forced to sell the castle. Finally the ghost finds peace and his descendant finds happiness in the arms of the millionaire's daughter.

*Like all the first films, THE CAT AND THE CANARY and THE GHOST GOES WEST are in black-and-white. For many people, black-and-white is far creepier than color. Judge for yourself.*

**THE GHOST GOES WEST, and so does his castle.**

# GHOSTLY GIGGLES

**M**oviemakers were quick to realize that as well as scaring you out of your wits, ghosts could tickle your ribs till you nearly died of laughter.

## GIGGLE RATING

| | |
|---|---|
| BLITHE SPIRIT | 💀💀💀💀💀 |
| BLACKBEARD'S GHOST | 💀💀 |
| GHOST DAD | 💀 |
| CASPER | 💀💀💀 |

**STAR CHOICE**

**7:00 P.M.** In **BLITHE SPIRIT** (1945), an eccentric medium, a suave novelist, his prim second wife, and the mischievous ghost of his glamorous first wife team up for one of the funniest of all ghost movies. Not only is this film based on a witty play by Noel Coward, but it also stars that old smoothie Rex Harrison as the novelist and the brilliantly batty Margaret Rutherford as the medium.

Join hands and meet the beautiful BLITHE SPIRIT who loves to make trouble.

**9:00** P.M. **BLACKBEARD'S GHOST** (1968, G) is one of Disney's craziest films. Peter Ustinov is the ghost of the notorious pirate. He is fated to haunt the deep until he does one good deed to make up for his wicked past. The good deed turns out to be saving a sleepy inn from plans for a ritzy new casino.

**11:00** P.M. **GHOST DAD** (1990, PG) stars famous TV sitcom dad, Bill Cosby. When an overworked widower is killed in a taxi accident, his ghost has just three days to sort out his finances for his three children. It's all a bit sentimental, but Bill Cosby's fans will love it.

**1:00** A.M. **CASPER** (1995, PG) is the friendly ghost of a boy. He lives in Whipstaff Manor with the ghosts of his three outrageous uncles—Stretch, Stinkie, and Fatso—who can't stand humans.

GHOST DAD's in a hurry.

This is bad news for ghost buster James Harvey and his daughter, Kat. They've been hired by Whipstaff's money-grabbing owner to evict the ghosts. The special effects really are special, mixing live action with amazing animation. And Casper is so adorable you'll want to take him home.

**Lonely CASPER makes friends with Kat.**

In **BLACKBEARD'S GHOST** the 17th-century outlaw meets a 20th-century lawman.

# GHOSTS ON THE RAMPAGE

**M**urder and mayhem (and a megahit called GHOSTBUSTERS). Do not watch these on your own.

Dan Aykroyd, Bill Murray, and Ernie Hudson are GHOSTBUSTERS.

**STAR CHOICE**

9:00 P.M. **GHOSTBUSTERS** (1984, PG) was one of the blockbusters of the mid–1980s. Three ghostbusters armed with fantastic special effects make a living ridding homes and offices of whatever haunts them. The story builds to a fabulous climax when they are hired to exorcise a New York apartment building built over the doorway to the spirit world.

7:00 P.M. **THE GHOST OF FRANKENSTEIN** (1942) provides just over an hour of pure terror. Master of horror Bela Lugosi plays Dr. Frankenstein's witless servant, Igor. The monster created by the sinister doctor gets a brain transplant from Igor and goes on the rampage. This is one of several Frankenstein movies, and one of the creepiest.

THE GHOST OF FRANKENSTEIN rises again.

| WHITE-WATER RATING | |
|---|---|
| THE GHOST OF FRANKENSTEIN | 💀💀 |
| GHOSTBUSTERS | 💀💀💀💀 |
| BEETLEJUICE | 💀💀💀💀 |

The 1989 sequel, *GHOSTBUSTERS II*, wasn't as good. So insist on the original—it's faster, funnier, and scarier.

*11:00 P.M.* In **BEETLEJUICE** (1988, PG) special effects run amok when a ghastly family moves into a new home and finds that it is haunted by the previous owners, Alec Baldwin and Geena Davis. But these ghosts are having difficulty being scary. To get rid of the humans, they call in Michael Keaton, bio-exorcist from hell. Hang on to your seats!

Michael Keaton dresses to kill in BEETLEJUICE.

BEETLEJUICE again, sitting pretty with an Oscar for Best Makeup.

# GHOSTS IN LOVE

**M**ovie ghosts have feelings too. When they fall in love, or come back to be with the loved ones they can't bear to leave behind, you'll reach for your hankies!

Drowning in kisses in A CHINESE GHOST STORY.

*7:00 P.M.* **A CHINESE GHOST STORY** (1987) has English subtitles, so bring your glasses. A young man falls in love with a beautiful ghost who happens to be a murderess controlled by a flesh-eating monster! The film is scary, funny, and touching, and the special effects are dazzling.

## SMOOCHY RATING

| | |
|---|---|
| A CHINESE GHOST STORY | 💀💀 |
| THE GHOST AND MRS. MUIR | 💀💀 |
| GHOST | 💀💀💀💀 |
| TRULY MADLY DEEPLY | 💀💀 |

**9:00 P.M.** **THE GHOST AND MRS. MUIR** (1947) is a wonderful tearjerker. Rex Harrison plays the sharp-tongued but tender-hearted ghost of Captain Daniel Gregg. He haunts the remote cliff-top cottage where Lucy Muir, a beautiful widow, and her daughter live. When the Captain begins to make his presence felt, Lucy demands that he appear.

The love story that unfolds is one of the most tender and most haunting ever filmed. It ends when the Captain realizes their love cannot be and whispers to the sleeping Mrs. Muir that it has all been a dream.

*THE GHOST AND MRS. MUIR get acquainted.*

**STAR CHOICE**

**11:00 P.M.** **GHOST** (1990, PG-13) won two Oscars and became one of the biggest box-office draws of the 1990s.

Heartthrob Patrick Swayze stars as a murdered banker who can't find peace until he tells his girlfriend, Molly, that he loves her and saves her from the clutches of his murderer. Demi Moore is the girlfriend, and Whoopi Goldberg is the bogus medium who never expected to meet a real ghost. The film is mushy, funny, exciting —and there's a terrific fight between Swayze and another ghost on the New York subway.

*Getting close again in GHOST.*

**1:30 A.M.** **TRULY MADLY DEEPLY** (1991, PG) is another topnotch ghostly tearjerker. Nina (Juliet Stevenson) is in deep mourning for Jamie, her dead cellist boyfriend. His ghost (Alan Rickman) comes back to play duets with her. Which is fine by her until he invites some other ghosts to join them. When these shivering shades move in, turn the heat up, and watch videos day and night, Nina wonders what she has gotten herself into.

*TRULY MADLY DEEPLY in love, with music.*

# CLASSICAL GHOSTS

**M**oviemakers sometimes turn to classic books and plays as a source of inspiration . . .

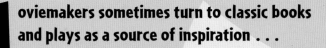

**STAR CHOICE**

**7:00 P.M. HAMLET** (1990, PG) features the oldest of our movie ghosts. It's based on William Shakespeare's tragedy, first staged in 1601. Hamlet is the young prince of Denmark. The ghost is his father. He tells Hamlet he was murdered by his brother, who then stole his crown and his widow. Hamlet must take revenge.

In this version (there are lots), Mel Gibson of LETHAL WEAPON fame makes a fine Hamlet.

**9:30 P.M. THE CANTERVILLE GHOST** (1944) comes from Oscar Wilde's witty story, first published in 1887. Charles Laughton plays the 16th-century ghost so timid he's scared of his own footsteps. A louse all his life, he has to haunt his house until he performs a heroic deed. With the help of Virginia, his descendant, he finally succeeds. Look out for later versions, too. David Niven and Sir John Gielgud had a lot of fun with this role.

| LONG-LIFE RATING | |
| --- | --- |
| HAMLET | 💀💀💀💀💀 |
| THE CANTERVILLE GHOST | 💀💀 |
| A CHRISTMAS CAROL | 💀💀💀💀 |

HAMLET (right) steels himself to avenge the murder of his father (above).

*11:30 P.M.* **A CHRISTMAS CAROL** by Charles Dickens was first published in 1843. It has become one of Hollywood's favorite ghost stories.

The first movie version was SCROOGE (1935), with Seymour Hicks in the title role. Then A CHRISTMAS CAROL (1951), a classic version starring Alastair Sim. Then another CHRISTMAS CAROL (1984, PG), this time with George C. Scott.

Here's the story they all tell. Scrooge is a tight-fisted, mean-spirited miser. He is awakened on Christmas Eve by the ghost of his former partner, Jacob Marley, and by the three spirits of Christmas past,

present, and future. So horrified is Scrooge when he sees what fate has in store that he finally changes his cold-hearted ways. Which is good news for his long-suffering employee, Bob Cratchit.

George C. Scott refuses to join in the festive spirit for A CHRISTMAS CAROL.

*And if that's not enough, two more versions of this Yuletide tale are showing next door on Screen Six.*

# MUSICAL GHOSTS

**A** CHRISTMAS CAROL is set to music and the show goes on. Is Charles Dickens turning in his grave, or clicking his fingers and tapping his feet?

**Kermit helps Michael Caine lighten up in THE MUPPET CHRISTMAS CAROL.**

Alec Guinness (left) shows Albert Finney the error of his ways in SCROOGE.

**STAR CHOICE**

*7:00 P.M.* **THE MUPPET CHRISTMAS CAROL** (1992, G) is simply irresistible! This musical version of Dickens's classic story stars Kermit and Miss Piggy as Mr. and Mrs. Cratchit, Michael Caine as Scrooge, and Muppets here, there, and everywhere. It also has an especially effective Ghost of Christmas Past, a larger-than-life Ghost of Christmas Present, and a chilling Ghost of Christmas To Come.

*9:00 P.M.* **SCROOGE** (1970, G) is another all-singing, all-dancing version of A CHRISTMAS CAROL. It got four Oscar nominations: Best Score, Best Song ("Thank You Very Much"), Best Costumes, and Best Art Direction.

This time Albert Finney takes the title role, and a gloriously spooky Alec Guinness is the grisly ghost of Jacob Marley. In one memorable scene, the old miser joins some happy revelers, unaware they are celebrating his funeral—he is dancing on his own coffin, and is about to be wound in chains and sent to Hell for all time. Will he repent in time?

---

### SONG & DANCE RATING

| | |
|---|---|
| THE MUPPET CHRISTMAS CAROL | ☠☠☠ |
| SCROOGE | ☠☠☠ |

✳

# SOB STORY

**T**HE **FRIGHT NIGHT** feast ends with a special treat, a large slice of all-American pie.

This field of corn turns into a **FIELD OF DREAMS** for Kevin Costner.

*7:00 P.M.* **FIELD OF DREAMS** (1989, PG) is for everyone who loves a happy ending. Ray Kinsella, a debt-ridden farmer played by Kevin Costner, gives in to spooky voices and plows up his land to build a baseball field. Then Ray's long-dead father and the ghosts of legendary players step out of the corn to play ball.

But will people come and buy tickets to the ghostly game? "They will come," says Ray's daughter, and they do, in droves. The farm is saved.

## GOOD SPORT RATING

**FIELD OF DREAMS**    |    ☠☠☠

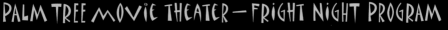

PALM TREE MOVIE THEATER—FRIGHT NIGHT PROGRAM

**CANDLEWICK PRESS**

READY REFERENCE

# HAUNTED HISTORY

**Ghosts go way back in time. The oldest ones come from folktales handed down by word of mouth over many centuries. With each invention of writing, printing, and computers, the number of ghost reports has soared.**

**O**ne of the earliest reports we have is almost 2,000 years old. A letter from Pliny, a Roman writer, tells of a house with a ghost that showed up every night moaning and clanking its chains. A new tenant by the name of Athenodorus noticed that the ghost vanished in the courtyard. When he hired some men to dig there, they found a skeleton in chains. The bones got a new burial, and the hauntings ceased.

**c. 3500 B.C.** Sumerians invent writing. Now hauntings can be recorded for posterity.

**c. 1200 B.C.** A ghost in Egypt asks for his tomb to be tidied up.

**490 B.C.** Greek and Persian armies meet at Marathon. Ghostly soldiers and horses relive the battle.

**40 B.C.** Athenodorus lays a ghost to rest in Athens, Greece.

**A.D. 900** Phantom Vikings raid the Abbey of Iona, Scotland.

**1483** The "two princes," 12-year-old Edward V and his brother Richard, are murdered in and haunt the Tower of London.

**1500s** A Dutch captain loses his ship off the Cape of Good Hope, Africa. Its ghost begins to roam the world. Sailors call it the *Flying Dutchman.*

**1748** The *Lady Luvibund* sinks in the English Channel. Its ghost resurfaces every 50 years. ▼

**1752** The *Palatine* runs aground on Block Island, in Long Island Sound, and is set on fire. Its phantom warns of stormy weather ahead.

**1815** A month after Napoleon's defeat at the Battle of Waterloo in Belgium, ghostly troops are seen fighting in the sky.

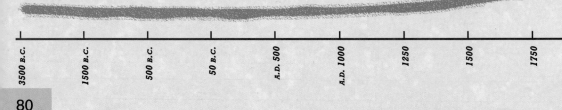

3500 B.C.    1500 B.C.    500 B.C.    50 B.C.    A.D. 500    A.D. 1000    1250    1500    1750

**1837** Joe Grimaldi, a clown, haunts the Theatre Royal in London, England.

**1848** The Fox sisters "talk" with their first ghost, New York, NY.

**1851** Students at Cambridge University in England set up the world's first ghost society.

**1861** William Mumler takes the first spirit photos, Boston, MA.

**1863** Ghosts in Civil War uniforms are seen at Gettysburg, PA, where 23,000 men were killed or wounded.

**1866** The annual phantom of Abraham Lincoln's

funeral train is first seen, Illinois. ▲

**1886** The phantom of a Maori war canoe appears on a lake in New Zealand, just before a nearby volcano erupts.

**1901** Two tourists in Versailles see Marie Antoinette, Queen of France, who was beheaded in 1793.

**1916** A ghostly sailor is sighted on a German U-boat in World War I.

**1929** Harry Price starts to investigate Borley Rectory, England.

**1964** Racing driver Donald Campbell sees his father's ghost in Australia, during a tense bid for a new world speed record.

**1972** After Flight 401 crashes in Florida, the ghostly crew are seen on other planes.

**1980s** A poltergeist is reported at a Toys Я Us™ store in California.

**1998** The *Lady Luvibund* fails to show. Is this the end of ghosts? No, hundreds of sightings are reported on the Internet every year.

**Will you and I be the ghosts of the future?**

Notice how ghosts keep up with the times. Once they haunted battlefields and ships. Now it's shops and planes. Where next?

*TIDAL WAVE*

*FLOOD*

*TRICKLE OF GHOST REPORTS*

1800  1825  1850  1875  1900  1925  1950  1975  2000 +

# GHOSTS AROUND THE GLOBE

**In the past, every country had its own local species of ghost. Nowadays these species are so rare they may be extinct.**

**NORTH AMERICA** Native Americans who suddenly acquired fame and fortune were suspected of being possessed by ghosts.

**IRELAND** Banshees are beautiful female spirits who sing mournfully to foretell a death in the family.

clack

click

clack

**MEXICO** At the beginning of November, Mexicans celebrate the Day of the Dead. Food, drink, and flowers are laid out for the spirits of the dead, and people dress up as skeletons and dance through the streets.

**CARIBBEAN** Zombies are dead bodies without a spirit, that are brought back to life by evil sorcerers to be their slaves.

**ENGLAND AND SCOTLAND**
Ghosts who do domestic chores are known as silkies and are treated with respect.

**RUSSIA** A domovoy is another ghost that does the housework, provided you treat it well.

**CHINA** A "hopping ghost" is so stiff with decay that it can only move by hopping along. It's so rotten that its smell can kill you.

phfaW!

**JAPAN** Shojo ghosts haunt the ocean. They don't mind humans, and they love offerings of sake (rice wine), so sailors don't mind having them around.

**NEW ZEALAND** Maori ghosts speak only to magicians, in whistles and squeaks.

aaahh!

**CENTRAL AFRICA**
Someone who dies in the bush and is left without a proper grave may come back as a ghost called an obambo. Relatives quickly build it a new hut and give it a funeral.

**INDIA** Hindus who die violently or don't get a proper funeral may come back as bhuts. These ghosts are especially mean to newly-weds, women and children.

# GHOST LORE

**Some people will do anything to meet a ghost. Others will do anything to avoid one. Here are some age-old tips for both.**

## LURES

◉ *Crossroads* Ghosts often haunt crossroads, maybe because murderers used to be hanged and buried there. If there's a crossroad near you, keep your eyes peeled.

◉ *Silver* Ghosts are particularly fond of this metal, so wear lots of silver jewelry.

◉ *Sage* Ghosts can't resist this herb. Pick some and keep it handy.

◉ *Second sight* Ask your mother when you were born. Babies born between midnight and 1 A.M. have the power to see ghosts.

◉ So does the seventh child of the seventh child. Do you have six older brothers and sisters? Does your mother or father?

## CURES

◉ *Daylight* The easiest way to get rid of ghosts is to wait. By dawn most of them fade away. Otherwise turn on all the lights. Bad spirits detest being in well-lit places.

◉ *Salt* Ghosts can't abide salt. Sprinkle some across your doorstep to keep them out of your home.

◉ *Silk* Ghosts are also allergic to silk. Wear a silk scarf to avoid being haunted.

◉ *Running water* Ghosts cannot cross running water. If you need to get away from one, wade through a stream.

◉ *Prayers* Try this old Cornish chant: *From ghoulies and ghosties and long-legged beasties, and things that go bump in the night, Good Lord, deliver us!*

# GHOSTS ONLINE

**If you don't trust ghost lore, the best source of information about ghosts these days is the Internet.**

## INTERNET GHOSTS

There are LOTS of websites about ghosts. Some of the most sane and easy to use are:

**Ghost Stories** A friendly discussion group that swaps stories, theories, and experiences of ghosts. You can just browse, or you can join in and chat.

 *alt.folklore.ghost-stories*

**Obiwan's UFO-Free Paranormal Page** A wonderfully busy website stuffed with over 500 ghost reports, loads of ghost information, answers to FAQs (Frequently Asked Questions), and links to other spooky sites.

☞ *http://www.ghosts.org*

**The Shadowlands: Ghosts and Hauntings** Hundreds of ghost reports, tips on ghost hunting, and links to other ghost sites. Perfect for beginners.

☞ *http://theshadowlands.net/ghost*

**Yahoo** An easy-to-use search engine that's great for tracking down ghost sites—it lists hundreds. Just type "ghosts" and you'll be away.

☞ *http://www.yahoo.com*

## GHOST SOCIETIES

Ghost societies all over the world investigate interesting hauntings. Here are two with good websites:

**SPIRIT** *(Society for Paranormal Investigation, Research and Informational Training)* Really well organized, and great for chatting to other ghost hunters.

☞ *http://www.ghosthunter.org*

**Australian Ghost Hunters Society** Shares its latest investigations and photos, as well as other reports and reviews of ghost tours and books.

☞ *http://homepages.tig.com.au/ ~aghs*

# GLOSSARY

**APPARITION** Something that appears unexpectedly and for which there seems to be no natural explanation. In other words, a ghost.

**CYBERGHOST** An abandoned website. With no one left to maintain them, these clutter up the Internet and lure innocent surfers to send e-mails that never get a reply.

**CYCLIC GHOST** A ghost that reappears on the anniversary of a significant event.

**DOPPELGANGER** German for "double walker," the identical image of a living person. If you meet your own doppelganger, hard luck! It's an omen of disaster or death.

Yikes

**ECTOPLASM** A substance that emerges from the body of spiritualist mediums as proof they are in touch with the forces of the great beyond.

**GHOST CRABS** Not spooky at all. Ordinary beach crabs of the Atlantic coast with a sandy-white color that reminds people of ghosts.

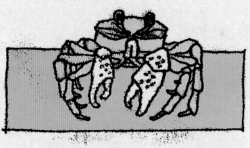

**GHOST TOWN** A town with no people. For example, Barkerville in Canada was once a gold-rush town with 10,000 people. When the gold ran out, they all drifted away, leaving only empty streets and doors slamming in the wind. Spooky but not necessarily haunted.

**MEDIUM** A person who claims to be able to help spirits get in touch with the world of the living. Does not usually speak to a ghost directly, but acts as a channel (perhaps by going into a trance) so the spirit can talk.

**PARANORMAL** An event that is unusual (like the figure of a Roman soldier in the 20th century . . .) and can't be explained by the laws of nature (. . . marching through a wall).

**POLTERGEIST** The German word for "noisy spirit." Poltergeists slam doors, throw things around, make phones ring, and so on. Sometimes they speak or move around like trapped wild animals.

**PSYCHIC INVESTIGATOR** A person who studies paranormal events to determine what causes them and whether they are real or fake. In other words, a ghost hunter.

**SÉANCE** A meeting held by spiritualists in order to contact the spirit world. Most séances are for the benefit of clients who pay good money for the chance to talk to someone in the afterlife.

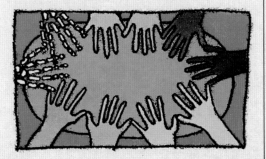

**SPIRIT MESSAGES** Spoken or written messages, or even messages sent in code, that are said to come from a ghost.

I AM A GHOST

**SPIRIT PHOTOGRAPHY** Pictures of alleged ghosts. They may show a clear human figure, or a shadowy form where the camera has caught what is claimed to be a spirit.

**SPIRITUALIST** Someone who believes that a human spirit can exist outside the body. They also believe that after a person dies their spirit can still express itself— usually by getting in touch with a medium.

**SUPERNATURAL** See paranormal.

OTHER WORDS FOR "GHOST":
apparition, phantom, shade, specter, spirit, spook
OTHER TYPES OF GHOST:
see pages 23–27

87

# INDEX

# ACKNOWLEDGMENTS

## PERMISSIONS

**Author and publisher would like to thank the following:**

**A.P. Watt Ltd. and Mrs. Sheila Reeves** for permission to abridge "The Empty House" by Algernon Blackwood, which first appeared in *The Empty House and Other Ghost Stories* (Eveleigh Nash, 1906).

**Matt Hucke** for permission to adapt "Ghost in Cemetery" from *www.graveyards.com/bachelors* and *Graveyards of Chicago* (Lake Claremont Press).

**Becky Richardson** for permission to adapt "The Haunted Café" from an article on *www.entertain.com/wedgwood/ghost*

**GolfWeb** for permission to adapt "Spooky" from an item by Eric Yoder on *www.golfweb.com/library/yoder/yoder961031*

**W.B. Herbert** for permission to adapt "Phantom Motorcyclist" from "The Newty Pond Motorbike," first published in *Railway Ghosts & Phantoms* © 1989 W.B. Herbert (David and Charles).

Every effort has been made to trace the ownership of all copyright material and to secure the necessary permission to adapt or reprint the material used herein. In the event of any question arising as to the use of any material, the publisher, while expressing regret for any inadvertent error, will be happy to make the necessary correction in future printings.

Although Dee Bunker investigates real ghost reports, please note that they have been adapted for her scrapbook, and that Dee and her case notes are a work of fiction.

## LONELY HEARTS

♥ **Ghost Hunter**, age 29, seeks ghost. *P.O. Box 398*

♥ **Is there anybody there?** Clairvoyant searching for a soul mate. *P.O. Box 478*

♥ **Shady, skeletal specter**, age 265, seeks special friend to rattle his chains. *P.O. Box 283*

♥ **Phantom pen pal** available for long-distance spirit rapping, automatic writing, etc. Fluent in all languages + Double Dutch. *P.O. Box 563*

♥ **Lonely, looking for love?** Tubby Tudor ghost, Henry, seeks 7th wife. *c/o Hampton Court.*

♥ **Lost your heart and your head?** *Apply to the Tower of London.*

## DIAL-A-GHOST

Perk up your party, horrify your boss, or wake up your neighbors. Phantoms to go, for any occasion.
Ghostline 555-1234

## PHOTOGRAPHS

**The Bridgeman Art Library** BL 22654 Battle of Culloden, April 16, 1746, British Library, p.34; BAL 51352 St. Louis pronouncing judgment, by G. Ge Saint Pathus (ms), Bibliothèque Nationale, p.51
**Mary Evans Picture Library** pp.52, 54l & r, 57tl & b, 58t, 59r; College of Psychic Studies Collection p.58b; Harry Price Collection pp.56, 57r; Captain Provand & Indra Shiva p.1; Peter Underwood Collection pp.52, 53
**Fortean Picture Library** Joanne Crowther p.60r; Marina Jackson p.60tl; Tony Vaci p.60bl
**Frank Lane Picture Agency** D. Hoadley p.33; David Hosking p.32
**Ghost Research Society** Dale Kaczmarek (President of the Ghost Research Society) p.36
**The Hulton Getty Picture Collection Limited** pp.23, 28, 39
**The Kobal Collection** 20th Century Fox p.73t; BBC Films/Film Four p.73b; MGM p.75t; Gill Distribution Ltd. p.74t; UIP p.67t; UIP/Amblin p.69bl; UIP/Gordon p.78
**The Ronald Grant Archive** 20th Century Fox p.77; American International Pictures p.50; Columbia p.70t; Enterprise Pictures Ltd. p.75b; Film Workshop Company/Cinema City/

Metro Pictures Ltd. p.72; Gill Distribution Ltd. p.74b; London Films p.67b; Paramount p.73m; Two Cities/Cineguild p.68t & b; UIP pp.66, 69t, 70b, 89; UIP/Amblin p.23; Walt Disney p.69br; Walt Disney/Jim Henson Organization p.76t & b; Warner Brothers p.71t & b
**Superstock** p.59bl
**Tony Stone Worldwide** Jean-François Causse p.41
**John Topham Picture Library** p.54m

## ILLUSTRATIONS

**Beth Aves** pp.2-4, 21, 30, 36-37, 40, 45tl, 90
**Simon Bartram** (Arena) pp.24-27, 38tr
**Lesley Buckingham** (Central Illustration Agency) pp.47-62
**Anders Lindholm** (Jacqui Figgis) pp.7-20
**Martin Macrae** (Folio) p.29
**Katherine Redfern** pp.79-92
**Ian Thompson** pp.22, 27tr, 32, 33, 35, 36-37, 40t, 42-43, 44-45, 46
**Peter Visscher** p.5

## CREDITS

Edited by
**Camilla Hallinan**
Designed by
**Beth Aves**
Cover design by
**Jonathan Hair**

Text pp. 1-4, 21-62 & 81-92 © 1999 by Christopher Maynard
Text pp. 5-20 this abridgement © 1999 by Walker Books Ltd.
Text pp. 63-80 © 1999 by Michael Johnstone
Illustrations © 1999 by Walker Books Ltd.

First U.S. paperback edition 2000

Library of Congress Cataloging-in-Publication Data is available.

Library of Congress Catalog Card Number 99-11358

ISBN (hardcover)
0–7636–0758–4
ISBN (paperback)
0–7636–1114–X

10 9 8 7 6 5 4 3 2 1

Printed in Hong Kong

Candlewick Press
2067 Massachusetts Ave.
Cambridge, MA 02140